"Stupendous! This book has it all: from the basics and building blocks of creating a great story to the spit-and-polish techniques so necessary for marketability. There's nothing like it anywhere."

— DEBORAH LEVINE HERMAN,
LITERARY AGENT, THE JEFF HERMAN AGENCY

"There's great wisdom in Diane O'Connell's Novel-Maker's Handbook, *and it's an excellent resource for anyone who wants to write a novel. Her step-by-step process for structuring a story will save you years of floundering. Her insights will help turn your dream of marketing success into a reality."*

— KRISTEN VON KRIESLER,
BESTSELLING AUTHOR OF *AN UNEXPECTED GRACE*

"If you're looking for a good practical guide for writing your novel, get a copy of Diane O'Connell's The Novel-Maker's Handbook. *All the basics of getting your story into final manuscript form are here, written in a clear, succinct, and friendly style. Breaking down the essential elements of a marketable novel, she offers valuable tips to apply to your own work and exercises to motivate your writing, whether you're just beginning or are stuck mid-way through or are looking to fine-tune your manuscript. An excellent resource for aspiring novelists."*

— GARY BRAVER,
BESTSELLING AND AWARDING-WINNING AUTHOR OF *TUNNEL VISION*

"This comprehensive guide offers everything that new or struggling writers need to know about all aspects of their story before struggling (and possibly failing). Recommended!"

— CHRIS ROERDEN,
NATIONAL AWARD-WINNING AUTHOR OF *DON'T SABOTAGE YOUR SUBMISSION* AND *DON'T MURDER YOUR MYSTERY*

THE NOVEL-MAKER'S HANDBOOK

the no-nonsense guide to crafting a marketable story

DIANE O'CONNELL

STATION
SQUARE
MEDIA

NEW YORK, NEW YORK

THE NOVEL-MAKER'S HANDBOOK: the no-nonsense guide to crafting a marketable story

Published by Station Square Media
16 West 23rd Street, 4th Floor
New York, NY 10010

Contributing Writer: Brianna Flaherty

Editor: Olga Vezeris
Cover Design: Kathi Dunn
Interior Design: Steven Plummer
Production Management: Janet Spencer King

Printed in the United States of America for Worldwide Distribution
ISBN: 978-0-9907250-4-6

Electronic editions:
Mobi ISBN: 978-0-9907250-5-3
epub ISBN: 978-0-9907250-6-0

First Edition

DEDICATION

for Larry

ACKNOWLEDGEMENTS

I OWE A DEBT of gratitude to the following people, for ensuring that this book actually got written and out into the world:

Brianna Flaherty, for writing the sample works-in-progress within the pages of this book, and for her impeccable research. Her wonderful writing skills, coupled with her willingness to allow others to view the process, have made this book so much more helpful to writers than it might otherwise have been.

My author clients, who so generously contributed their insights and excerpts: Carolyn Kay Brancato, Tom Farrell, Dale Funk, Cody McFadyen, Matt McMahon, Hank Pasinski, Katherine Rapp, Jennifer Snell, Khaled Talib, and Joanne Tombrakos.

Olga Vezeris, whose razor-sharp editing helped make this book one I can be truly proud of, and to my superb production team: production manager Janet Spencer King, cover designer Kathi Dunn, marketing genius Graham van Dixhorn, copyeditor Linda Dolan, interior designer Steven Plummer, and indexer and proofreader Jane Scott.

Cristina Schreil, *The Novel-Maker's Handbook*'s executive editor, for keeping me on track, on task, in good spirits, and for generating quite a lot of blog content that ultimately made it into the book.

A special thanks to Deborah Levine Herman for her unwavering support and insisting I write this book.

Finally, to my husband Larry, who has never stopped believing in me and has always pushed me out of my comfort zone to stretch my wings.

TABLE OF CONTENTS

Part II: Refining Your Draft

Part III: Committing to Yourself as a Writer

WHY I WROTE THIS BOOK

I N MY WORK over the years with authors, both as an editor for major publishing companies and as a book development expert in my own business, I have seen too many authors struggle for years to get a draft done, only to find out that their story is not strong enough, or the characters are weak, or the structure is off. Often, they had come to me after collecting a stack of rejection letters from agents. I knew there had to be a better way—a way that would get them to a publishable draft in a much shorter time. So, I began to work with authors at the beginning of the writing process—instead of after they had completed multiple drafts.

What developed out of my work with these authors was truly remarkable: they were able to write a draft with ease. Not only that, but because they had learned how to build a novel the right way — through a step-by-step process that lays a solid foundation for the story *before* beginning to write — they were actually able to circumvent the problems that many first-time authors get into with their early drafts.

I know this process works because I've used it in my own work. A number of years ago I got a contract to write a biography about a highly accomplished physicist for a series of books profiling women scientists. I had a very short time in which to write the book and submit it. So, after spending a good deal of that time interviewing my subject and others who knew her, not to mention learning everything I could about physics (I knew nothing), I found myself with a pile of information, but no story. And my time was running out. What to do? I was stuck. I didn't know how to tell my subject's story in a way that would show a clear journey and engage readers.

That's when I decided to forget about just sitting down to write. I would begin at the beginning—with a clear vision of what this book was going to be about—and then build out the story one step at a time. The process was revelatory; it took me less time to write this book than all the other ones I had written previously, the writing process was a lot less fraught, I had minimal revisions to make for the publisher, and even more gratifying, the book, *Strong Force: The Story of Physicist Shirley Ann Jackson*, became a bestseller in the series. So, I know this process works from both an editor's standpoint and an author's standpoint.

I began to refine that process by delving into the techniques that bestselling authors use to craft their novels. What developed was a clear step-by-step method, which I then used in my one-on-one work with authors to help them write their novels. I also presented this method around the country at writing conferences and in workshops. When I kept getting requests for a book from my author clients and workshop attendees, I knew that there was a strong need.

I could no longer put off writing this book.

My aim in this book is to help you—the aspiring novelist—learn how to write a novel so that you don't end up spending years spinning your wheels trying to construct a salable story and a well-crafted novel of which you can be proud.

HOW TO USE THIS BOOK

WHEN YOU READ a bestselling novel, the work can seem effortless. The characters and story seem almost inevitable, as if they sprang full force into being, insisting themselves upon the author. As a reader, you are so pulled into the world of the story that it may seem as though it had always been this way.

What you don't see are the gears: the intricate crafting it took to get the story in shape. You don't see the starts and stops, the characters or scenes that started out in the story only to be discarded like empty tuna cans when they became useless to the telling of the story. You don't see the clunky language that has now been so expertly smoothed over. What you see is simply a riveting story.

But how did the author get there?

Starting to write a novel is easy. You have the spark of an idea, a rush of creativity, and the flush of embarking on a new venture. But then reality kicks in. It may be after the first page, after the outline you so carefully crafted, or after the first few chapters. You realize that writing a novel is darn hard work. The scenes that were so vividly crafted in your head now have all the excitement of a technical manual. Dialogue that crackled in your mind now fizzles on the page. Action can feel as clunky as a toddler taking her first steps. And the plot, which seemed at first so logical, now reads more like the literary equivalent of a surrealist work of art. As the oft-repeated saying goes, "Writing is easy; you just sit at a typewriter and open a vein." Or as Dorothy Parker so succinctly put it, "I love having written."

> ## What dooms many writers from finishing what they started? Simple: they don't know *how* to write a novel.

So, what dooms many writers from finishing what they started? Simple: they don't know *how* to write a novel.

Now, I know there are many highly successful authors who write by the seat of their pants. There's even a term for it: "pantsers." And they are proud to call themselves that. I first heard this term in a writing workshop led by thriller writer, Steven James, author of numerous *New York Times* bestsellers, including *Singularity*. He is an avowed pantser.

Frankly, the idea of just sitting down to write whatever comes to mind scares the pants off some writers. Those are the "plotters," the ones who need to have everything figured out before they ever write the first scene. And there's a camp that says, "You need to know exactly where you'll end up before you should begin." As for me, both approaches feel inadequate for the first-time author.

The pantsers who are successful know instinctively how to create compelling characters and set them on a journey that continually raises the stakes. They seem to have an innate sense of story structure, whether that comes naturally or from years of writing drafts that are now collecting dust under their beds.

The plotters, on the other hand, may be the kind of people who are terrified of going down a dark path, unable to see what's next, let alone where they'll end up. They need to know where each step is leading. Alfred Hitchcock was legendary, not just for his brilliant films, but for having worked out every single shot before he ever arrived on the set. There was no room for deviation or "Hey, what if we tried it this way?" Still, that process worked for him. But what about the majority of writers? They may have created a tightly woven story only to discover that it lacks emotional resonance and that they have created characters who readers simply don't identify with.

So, what's the answer?

The process that unfolds in the following chapters will impose a little discipline on the pantser, and free up the creativity of the plotter.

In my experience I have found that most writers are a combination of pantser and plotter, switching between the two at various stages of writing. The method that I have developed is meant to bridge both approaches. The process that unfolds in the following chapters will impose a little discipline on the pantser and free up the creativity of the plotter. But more importantly, it will help you—whatever your natural inclination is—to complete your novel in as quick and painless a way as possible. This process can save literally years of writing in the dark, trying to find your story. It will cut down on the number of rewrites you will need to do to end up with a satisfying story.

But what if you already have a draft? You can use this method as a way to diagnose what may not be working, and to strengthen what is working. The techniques presented here will help you revise with clear intention.

And if you've started a draft but got stuck partway through, this process will help you figure out why you got stuck and give you the tools to work through those blocks.

No matter what stage you're in—whether birthing an idea or having written a complete draft—this book will work for you.

MAKING THIS BOOK WORK FOR YOU

This book is divided up into three parts.

Part I: Getting the Bare Bones Down, will help you complete a Working Draft of your novel. It will be messy and will need work to refine it, but it will have all the story elements and character relationships in place. You'll get your best results if you work through the chapters in this part chronologically.

Part II: Refining Your Draft, will help you put the meat on the bones, so to speak. You'll learn a step-by-step process for sharpening your scenes, your characters, and your overall story-telling skills. In Chapter 20, Anatomy of a Well-Engineered Scene, you'll see how all these elements come together to create a beautifully crafted scene.

Part III: Committing to Yourself as a Writer, will give you valuable advice for getting unstuck when the inevitable happens, handling external forces that impede your writing progress, learning to deal with rejection, and knowing when to hire and how to work with an editor.

Throughout the chapters, I've included voices from authors I've worked with, as well as some of my students, who have used these tools. They talk about their own experiences and how they have adapted these tools by putting their own spin on them. That's what I hope for you: that you will take the process I've laid out in this book, learn from it, adapt it to your needs, and make it your own.

This book is not meant to make you slavishly follow a "formula." It is not meant to change your voice. Every writer has his or her own authentic voice. This book will teach you how to craft a novel through a method that works—and can even be joyful.

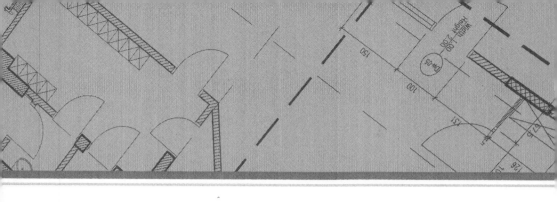

PART I

GETTING THE
BARE BONES DOWN

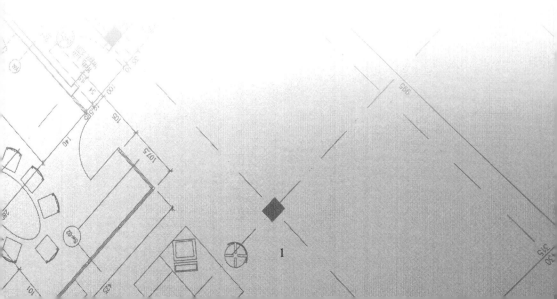

1

WHAT'S THE BIG PICTURE?

Clarifying the Vision for Your Story

WHENEVER I WORK with an author, one of the first things I ask is, "What is this story about?" It's a seemingly simple question, but one that stymies almost every beginning author.

Often, they will answer the question with some variation of the following:

"It's about some store-front lawyers."

"It's about a plot to take down the country's power grid."

"It's about a traveling circus during the Depression."

"It's a modern-day western."

All of these statements may be true, but they only reveal a small piece of the big picture. They do not reflect what the novel is really about. The problem in approaching your novel by concentrating on any one of the above descriptors, before you have a clear vision of what your story is about, is that you can end up with a structure that's all off, or a story that lays flat on the page, or a novel that spends too much real estate on exposition or dialogue or setting or plot at the expense of a tale well told.

Novels are not about *characters*—though you can't have a novel without them.

Novels are not about *what happens*—though you can't have a novel without stuff happening.

Novels are not about *setting*—though you must set your scenes in a place and time.

Novels are not about *genre*—though most novels fall into some kind of genre.

Novels are about something much bigger than each of the components. But first, all novels must start with a vision. It could be as simple as a photo that sparks an idea for a character, a visit to a place that inspires a setting for your story, or a "What if?" kind of question.

Mitch Albom's Uncle Eddie lay in a hospital battling a high fever. At one point, still delirious from fever, he woke to find all his dead relatives sitting at the edge of his bed. Albom's uncle's literal vision inspired Albom to ask a big "What if?" question, which became the vision for his novel, *The Five People You Meet in Heaven*. Inspiration for a story can strike as simply and unassumingly as that.

The vision can also begin with an incident from your own life. When Stieg Larsson was a teen, he failed to help an acquaintance who was being gang-raped. Though he begged her for forgiveness, she never gave him the absolution he so desperately needed. That incident haunted him and became the vision for his blockbuster trilogy that began with *The Girl with the Dragon Tattoo*.

While flipping through the channels late one night, Suzanne Collins caught a glimpse first of a reality TV competition and then of war footage on the news. The two images melded together overnight, and when she applied her thoughts to paper, the bestselling *The Hunger Games* trilogy was the end result.

When she was at the gym, Lauren Oliver contemplated a Gabriel García Márquez essay she'd just finished, in which the author claimed that all books are about either love or death. Having written her first book, *Before I Fall*, about death, Oliver was determined to write next about love. As she worked out, she also watched a news report about a pandemic, and her two streams of thought began to converge in her head. The resulting novel was *Delirium*, the first of Oliver's bestselling trilogy.

What happens in Lauren Oliver's books is a huge part of their draw. Like *The Hunger Games*, the dystopian setting of *Delirium* makes readers feel as if they are seeing a possible, albeit scary, glimpse of our world's future. Placing Lena Haloway at the helm of her story, Oliver elicits an emotional investment in the well-being of her young, innocent protagonist. Lena's character journey grips readers from the very first page, as she faces an impending, government-mandated procedure called the "Cure," which will remove her capacity to love. But *Delirium* is not ultimately about the Cure, or Lena Haloway, or the dystopian setting of the story. Instead, Oliver's novel strikes at the intersection of all these elements of story—it is the tale of a young woman coming to know herself for the first time, by combatting an oppressive government and fighting to assert what she believes is fair and just. To put the process simply: Lauren Oliver took a single vision and grew it into story.

THE BIG PICTURE

If you think of the vision as the spark that ignites the idea, the big picture is the flame that gives full expression to the story. The vision may be enough to start writing out your ideas, experimenting with plot lines, characters, or scenes, but you need to take a moment first to think about how you plan on turning that initial vision into a full-fledged novel. Writers like Stieg Larsson and Mitch Albom have a big-picture plan in mind long before they reach the end of the writing process. It doesn't matter whether you are halfway through a first draft, have just begun writing scenes, are still in the idea phase, or are even having to go back through an entire draft. Now is the time to take a moment to think about the big picture: what is your novel really about?

> The vision may be enough to start writing out your ideas, but you need to stop to think about how you plan on turning that initial vision into a full-fledged novel.

When confronted with this daunting question, I can hear the pantsers among you crying out to just sit down and write the darn thing and let the big picture reveal itself. And you plotters are probably figuring that knowing everything that happens along the way is enough to reveal the story. So, here's something to think about:

Imagine you wanted to build a house. If you're a pantser, you might be apt to start putting up walls and creating rooms as you feel inspired. Think of the disaster that could result: staircases leading nowhere, rooms that don't function, and a house that could flood or blow up because you didn't lay in the plumbing and electric the right way! But this is exactly the kind of thing that could happen if you approach writing your novel in the same way. You could end up writing plot lines that lead to nowhere, characters who repeat each other, and scenes that have no purpose.

A plotter who builds a house could end up with a perfectly constructed dwelling that has no warmth, no heart, no reflection of the people who live inside the walls. It's the same with approaching your novel that way. You could create a perfectly plotted story, but the characters may ring hollow, and the structure may be so forced that it leaves the reader in the dust.

Whether you're a pantser or a plotter, you don't start with the blueprint. You actually start way before that, by asking yourself what your vision for your house would be. Will it be a weekend cottage? A

> ## ORIGINAL VISION
>
> Do you know what your original vision was for your novel? Whether you are still searching for your idea, have just begun to flesh out your idea, or are even through a draft, now is the time to step back to review and ask a few questions:
>
> - Why was I drawn to this idea?
> - What was the initial spark?
> - What gets me excited about my novel?
> - What do I like most about my idea? (The characters, the setting, the emotions it stirs within me? A big moment?)
> - What *don't* I know yet about my story?
>
> Asking yourself these questions will help you begin to think about the whole of the novel rather than the bits and pieces. Plus, it will serve as a reminder as you get further along in your writing—and as it gets more difficult—of what you had in mind at the start. Whenever you feel like giving up, you can always refer back to that initial vision.

starter home? A home for a large, extended family? A house that will support a home-based business? Will it be sleek and modern, with an open floor plan and lots of windows to let in the natural light? Or would you prefer to have lots of separate rooms and a more womb-like feeling? Each of these structures has a different purpose and will be designed to suit that purpose.

To clarify your vision for your novel, you need to begin thinking about each of the components mentioned earlier: who your story is about, where and when your story is set, the big plot idea, and even the genre. All these components combined will help you to define what, exactly, your story is about.

WHO IS THIS STORY ABOUT?

To answer the question "What is this story about?" you first need to ask yourself, "*Who* is this novel about?" This is your main character: the protagonist, the hero (or heroine), the star, the pivotal character, the main actor, the primary person of interest. Now, you may have dozens of characters, and a few of them will be very important to the story. Maybe one or two will be very, very important. But there should be only one central character. Like it or not, you must prioritize! That goes whether you're writing in first person singular point of view (POV) or in multiple POVs.

> You may have dozens of characters, and a few of them will be very important to the story. But there should be only one central character.

To determine your main character, ask yourself:

Who is the driver of the story?

The main character must be active and affect the action. He may be reluctantly forced to take action, or he may dive into it willingly and wholeheartedly.

Who has the most to gain or lose?

The main character must have something very vital at stake: life or death, honor, love, vengeance, passion.

Who has the most obstacles to overcome?

It can't be easy for your character. He or she must be met with roadblocks at every step of the way.

Who changes the most from beginning to end?

You may have heard the term "hero's journey," popularized by Joseph Campbell. Your main character must have something internal to overcome: mistrust, inability to love, addiction, cynicism, etc. By the end of the story, she must be very different than she was at the beginning.

Let's take a look at how this would work in the now classic, bestselling 1974 novel *Jaws,* by Peter Benchley, which most people know through the blockbuster film by the same name.

In *Jaws*, there are three leading characters: Brody, the police chief; Hooper, the scientist; and Quint, a professional shark hunter. While each of these characters could potentially be seen as equal, there is clearly only one main character: Brody. Why?

Brody satisfies all of the questions above:

Brody is the driver of the story.

It is Brody who tries to force the town of Amity to close the beaches after the shark attack, and who ultimately persuades the mayor to pay Quint a hefty fee to pursue the shark and kill it.

Brody has the most to gain or lose.

Sure, Hooper and Quint also put their lives at risk when they set out on the Orca, but it's Brody who would leave behind a widow and two children.

Brody has the most obstacles to overcome.

He is an outsider, a police chief with no authority, and is afraid of the water. None of the other characters' obstacles even come close.

Brody changes the most from beginning to end.

By the novel's end, he has confronted his fear of the water, and is the one to vanquish the shark.

WHO IS THE OPPONENT?

Now that you know who your main character will be, you need to give her an opponent—someone who will make life more difficult for the main character, who will thwart her, who will challenge her, who will help her grow by the novel's end.

The opponent can be as obvious as the serial killer who seems to be outsmarting your main character detective at every turn or as subtle as a love interest who is emotionally unavailable. Don't let the term "opponent" throw you; an opponent doesn't necessarily mean the character is villainous. He or she can be someone who is sympathetic and supportive of the main character, but who pushes him through the journey.

Whoever your opponent is, be sure to give him traits that serve to reinforce your main character's journey. (We'll get into character journey and traits in Chapter 2.) In *Jaws*, for example, what better opponent for a character who is afraid of the water than a shark? This is an example of man against nature.

Whoever your opponent is, be sure to give him traits that serve to reinforce your main character's journey.

Let's look at some other examples:

Anyone can tell you that, in J. K. Rowling's series, Harry Potter's opponent is Lord Voldemort. Sure, Harry faces other forms of opposition—from the Dursley family, his peers, and the pressure to do well at Hogwarts. But simply by existing in contrast to Voldemort, who embodies evil, manipulation, and heartlessness, Harry begins to appear to the reader as a goodhearted, courageous underdog—which is precisely what he proves himself to be throughout each book. Harry's journey toward self-actualization and heroism is reinforced each time he confronts He-Who-Must-Not-Be-Named.

Identifying the opponent in a story can be tricky sometimes. And in some cases, the main character can also be the opponent: man against himself. Pat Bateman, the violent, mentally unstable protagonist in *American Psycho*, embodies both main character and main opponent in Bret Easton Ellis's novel. Though Bateman feels opposed by the seeming success and stability of his Wall Street peers, the crux of the novel is truly his destructive opposition against himself. He often questions his own obsession with material goods, critically examines his violent behavior, and—by aggravating his own internal discord—ultimately furthers his character's alienation and self-destruction.

In Cormac McCarthy's *The Road*, the unnamed man and his son are opposed by the post-apocalyptic landscape of the story, rather than a singular, specific character. Though they encounter individual opponents along the way, like the cannibalistic people roaming the countryside, their ultimate and consistent struggle is against the harsh and desolate environment. Like *Jaws*, this is a man against nature model. Through this opposition, their characters are conveyed to the reader as resilient, strong, and fiercely loyal to one another. In this way, McCarthy establishes a bond between the man and his son that deepens the emotional weight of the story as a whole. Without constant opposition, stories lose the critical tension that engages readers with the text.

To determine your main opponent, ask yourself:

- Who has the most to gain or lose besides the main character?

- Who can push the main character to his limits?

- Who can illuminate the main character's journey best by highlighting that character's flaws and/or needs?

- Who is strong enough in personality, desire, and abilities to be a formidable enough opponent to the main character?

WHAT IS THE SETTING?

Stories don't happen in a vacuum. Time and place affect events. An ambitious twenty-five-year-old African-American woman in Manhattan during the present day is going to have a very different set of experiences and challenges than an ambitious twenty-five-year-old African-American woman in Mississippi in 1960.

Setting can be as integral to the story as any of the characters. In many bestselling novels, the setting is almost what comes to mind first when we think of them: *Water for Elephants* (a traveling circus during the depression), *The Kite Runner* (Afghanistan during the 1970s), *2001: A Space* Odyssey (it's all there in the title). Could you imagine *Gone With the Wind* set in the Pacific Northwest? How about *Jane Eyre* set in San Francisco during the Summer of Love?

What would *Alice in Wonderland* be like if Wonderland was an urban metropolis?

Setting can be as integral to the story as any of the characters.

In *Jaws*, the setting is the fictional Long Island town of Amity: a beachside community that depends upon the tourists who come there during the summer. So, when does the first shark attack take place? Just before the start of the summer season. If just one of those facts about the setting had been changed—if it were set in late September or on a private beach—the story would not have the same impact.

WHAT IS THE CENTRAL CONFLICT?

Most people try to avoid conflict in their everyday lives. But conflict is precisely what novels need to succeed. It's why we read novels, go to the movies, see plays, watch TV. Think about it: no one wants to read a story about a carefree person with a charmed life who gets everything she wants and lives happily ever after. Even children's fairy tales are fraught with conflict and obstacles before we get to the happily ever after.

Conflict is the basis of all storytelling. Just look at these opening lines if you have any doubts:

- "All happy families are alike; each unhappy family is unhappy in its own way." —*Anna Karenina*, Leo Tolstoy

- "It was the best of times, it was the worst of times …" —*A Tale of Two Cities*, Charles Dickens

- "Not for the first time, an argument had broken out over breakfast at number four, Privet Drive." —*Harry Potter and the Chamber of Secrets*, J. K. Rowling

- "Harry locked his mother in the closet." —*Requiem for a Dream,* Hubert Selby, Jr.

- "When Gregor Samsa awoke one morning from troubled dreams he found himself transformed in his bed into a monstrous insect." —*The Metamorphosis*, Franz Kafka

Each of these opening lines conveys a promise to the reader: the road is not going to be easy for these characters. The central conflict will be either with their relationships, the society they live in, their outside opponents, or themselves.

Making the conflict big enough

One of the biggest problems I see with beginning novelists is that the central problem of their story is simply not big enough. I don't mean that they need to have the world coming to an end, or have stuff blowing up, or have bodies piling up—that's the stuff of Hollywood blockbusters, not novels. What I mean is that the conflict has to be something deep, tough to solve, and able to last an entire novel. In essence, it needs to be big enough for readers to care about.

The conflict has to be something deep, tough to solve, and able to last an entire novel.

For instance if you're writing a young adult romance and it's only about a nerdy boy who wants to date the hot girl, that's not a big enough problem. The reader will ask, "Who cares?" But if the nerdy boy's mom has just become engaged to the hot girl's dad, your story's conflict begins to expand.

If your main character longs to purchase a fixer-upper house on the wrong side of town, and could conceivably qualify for a mortgage, there's no real conflict there; the problem is easily solved. But what if he doesn't have a penny to his name and couldn't qualify for a loan on a cup of coffee, much less a house? Now he's got a seemingly insurmountable hurdle to get over, one that would presumably take a good part of the novel to find the solution.

The central conflict also has to be big enough to carry through an entire manuscript. A story cannot revolve entirely around the tough breakup of two characters in an isolated setting—not without drawing in external forces and characters (the other woman; the fact that they're still on the same lease and neither can afford to move out) to complicate and expand their relationship into a full manuscript.

In its most reduced form, Kathryn Stockett's *The Help* is about Skeeter living out her journalistic dreams by sneaking around to interview her town's maids. Not a terribly dramatic plot, right? But when you take into account the setting of the story—Jackson, Mississippi in the 1960s—the racial tension complicates the narrative immensely, as does Skeeter's decision to publish the stories she collects. The novel's scenes are then underscored with secrecy and the threat of violence and social upheaval at any moment. So, what might have originally been enough conflict for a mildly dramatic story about Skeeter's dreams of being a journalist easily becomes enough material for a fully realized novel.

BEFORE MOVING ON

You may be tempted to skip this step—especially if you have a general idea of what your story is about, or if you believe that it will eventually become apparent as you write. But take the time now to delve into your novel's vision. This is important not just for your character's journey, but also for your own journey as a writer. You'll thank yourself down the road, when things get messy and you're not sure which way to turn. Your Big Vision will act as your beacon to get to the end of the journey.

MAKING THE PITCH

What makes you buy a certain book? Think about the last time you were browsing in your local bookstore, or even an online bookstore. Unless you were there to buy a book that you had already determined you wanted, chances are you may have been attracted by the title, the book cover, maybe the author's name. All of those are what may have attracted you to consider the book further. But chances are, you turned the book over to read the back cover copy—or if it was a hardcover book, you read the "flap copy;" the copy inside the cover flap that tells you what the book is about.

It may seem premature to write the flap copy for your book before you even have a first draft done, but this is the easiest—and surest—way to sharpen your story's focus.

Creating the pitch for your book requires specificity—you must know what, ultimately, is at the core of your story that will make readers care about what you have to say. It may seem premature to write the flap copy for your book before you even have a first draft done, but this is the easiest—and surest—way to sharpen your story's focus. If you have any big weaknesses, this is the place where they will become readily apparent. It's also much easier to fix a fault line before you've gotten too far into the writing, when flaws will only grow to the point that the story may be irretrievably broken. And it's a great time-saver because you won't have to get to the end of a draft to learn that your story's gone off the rails.

How you write the flap copy is up to you, but it should answer the following questions:

1. **Who is your story about?**

2. **Who is the opponent?**

3. **What is the main conflict in your novel?** Is it to solve a crime, to find love, to uncover corruption, to defeat an enemy?

4. **What is the event that gets the story in motion?** I call this the Happening. (We will get into this in more detail in a later lesson.)

5. **What themes are you exploring?** For instance, is yours a story of love and loss? Of the corrosive effects of success? Of redemption?

Other Tips

Be sure to capture the tone of your novel. If it's a romantic comedy, keep the language light and funny; if it's a dark thriller, keep the language edgy and ominous.

Avoid clichés. If you use a cliché in your cover copy, chances are something in your story is also hackneyed.

Don't tell the whole story. Think of the flap copy as "teaser." It's just enough to get a reader interested in your story.

Think of the effect you want to have on readers. In a thriller, you want them to be tense, scared, on edge. In a drama, you want them to have a deep emotional experience. In a ghost story, you want to scare them. In an inspirational tale, you want them to be uplifted.

BEFORE MOVING ON

Take a few moments to craft your vision into the pitch for the novel. Write it out large enough, so you can't miss it. You might even want to incorporate it into a poster-sized Vision Board for your novel. Post it where you do your writing so it acts as a reminder of what your story is really about.

SAMPLE FLAP COPY

From *Dead Again* by Hank Pasinski

Phil Pason **[main character]** joined the DEA looking for an adventurous life and the chance to avenge the death of a friend destroyed by drug dealers. Now, fresh out of the Academy, rookie agent Pason is assigned to infiltrate The Scorpions and the Blanco Diablos **[the Happening]**—the two most dangerous and bloodthirsty drug gangs **[the opponents]** in the American Southwest **[the setting]**. Going deep undercover, he lives under false identities and gives up all contact with friends and family. He must rely on his wits, his courage, and a little bit of luck to avoid gruesome death if his true identity is ever discovered **[the main conflict]**. Along the way, he finds love in an unexpected place, and longs to return home to his small-town roots after his dangerous work is done. But will his enemies let him? *Dead Again* is the story of a small-town boy who longs for an adventurous life—and gets more than he bargained for **[theme]**.

WRITING THE FLAP COPY

Be sure to answer these questions:

1. Who is my story about?

2. Who is the main opponent?

3. What is the main conflict?

4. What is the event that gets the story in motion?

5. What themes am I exploring?

6. What tone do I want to capture?

7. What effect do I want to have on my readers?

2

CASTING CALL
Choosing Your Characters Wisely

IT'S SAID THAT readers can love stories—but only *fall* in love with characters. We root for them to succeed, feel crushed when they fail, hold our breath when they're in danger, breathe a sigh of relief when they escape unharmed, feel stirrings in our soul when the object of their desire reciprocates, and feel crushing betrayal when that same object of desire cheats on them.

Even the worst villains—if fully rendered—can provoke intense emotions. We fear them, we revile them, and we envy their cunning. We desperately wish for them to be defeated, and we feel a sense of satisfaction when they're vanquished—but we also feel just a little bit sad because we won't have the warped pleasure of their company any longer.

When you think of the classic novels that have endured through the ages, as well as the more recent bestsellers, what comes to mind? The characters. Scarlett O'Hara, Jane Eyre, Captain Ahab, Jay Gatsby, Harry Potter, Hannibal Lecter, and Lisbeth Salander all seem as real to us as if they had actually existed.

Too often, though, many of the first-time authors I've worked with know their characters only about as well as they would know an acquaintance at a cocktail party. Writers who fall into the pantser category often create characters whose traits and descriptions seem like ticks the author thought would be interesting, rather than ones that arise out of a deeply embedded worldview. Plotters, on the other hand, construct characters who act in ways that serve the author's preconceived ideas for plot, rather than driving the plot because of who they are. For plotters and pantsers alike, characterization tends to become tricky because the author has not taken the time to fully develop the novel's characters before thrusting them onto the page.

That's what this chapter will help you do. We will take a look at your characters and help you get to know them on a deeper level. Just as an architect creates a blueprint for a house before building, you must create a blueprint for your novel's characters. Start by asking a few questions:

- Who are they?

- How did they get to this place in your novel?

- What do they want?

- What's standing in their way?

HISTORY DETERMINES THE PRESENT

While you may have ideas for some colorful characters, you need to go back to way before your story ever starts to discover each character's history, or "backstory." Why? Because who we are is the accumulation of what has happened to us in the past—and how we have chosen to respond to those events.

Our experiences during our formative years shape *everything*, even if we try to leave behind the past and reinvent ourselves. They affect how we see the world—our lens—no matter how much we might have changed in the intervening years. You've probably heard the expression, "Wherever you go, there you are." That's exactly what is meant. Think of Lisbeth Salander in *The Girl with the Dragon Tattoo*. Everything about her, even the name she uses as a computer hacker—Wasp—says "keep away." She's odd, off-putting, weird to look at, and dresses as though she were going into battle. That all stems from a horribly traumatic past. It's the past that made her who she is in the present.

> ## Our experiences during our formative years affect how we see the world—our lens—no matter how much we might have changed in the intervening years.

I remember coming across a TV episode of *The Mentalist*. In one scene, a cop investigates the murder of a teen by first visiting her home. She conducts an interview with the father, who is understandably upset and traumatized. The cop observes a number of empty beer bottles on the coffee table and a house in disarray. She appears abrupt, even harsh in her questioning of the distraught father who, after all, just lost his only child.

When she leaves the house, she trips down the stairs of the front porch—an action that reveals that something more than the child's murder is on her mind. As you may have guessed, we learn that her own father was an abusive alcoholic. This character's history colors how she views the present situation and how she reacts to the father, as well as to her partner, who is dismayed at her harsh treatment of the bereaved father. She sees the world through the lens of an adult child of an alcoholic.

HOW HISTORY AFFECTS STORY

Knowing your characters' histories will help you determine what happens in your novel. In other words, history determines character, which in turn determines plot.

It's the history that affects how your character sees the world and responds to external forces. In turn, the external forces acting upon your character reveal your character's lens. Character and lens are as dependent upon each other as the strands of a hook-and-loop fastener. Each strand is useless on its own; together they form a strong bond. And they stay together—until an outside force acts on them to tear them apart.

Ultimately, the lens drives a character's actions and reactions, which drives the plot. Let's take a look at how this might work. Let's say you have an idealistic young man who believes that a good citizen stands up for his country's ideals ("My country, right or wrong"). That's his lens and he came to that because of his history. And that way of thinking and seeing the world drives him to enlist in the army when the United States goes to war with Iraq. So, we have the *lens* (idealistic), the *external force* (a war), and *the character's response* to that external force (enlisting in the army). Are you following me?

History determines character, which in turn determines plot.

Now, let's say that when he's in Iraq fighting, he sees some things that cause him to question his country's role in the war. He's a witness to torture, maybe sees innocent children being slaughtered. He becomes disillusioned, maybe even angry. He's still the same *character*, but his lens has changed due to the *external forces*; therefore, his actions will change. He may go AWOL, he may turn in a superior officer, he may leak classified information to the press, or he may bottle up his rage and take it out on his wife when he returns home.

DRAWING UP A CHARACTER BLUEPRINT

Knowing your character's history is only the first step to creating fully fleshed-out characters. To begin the process of creating multidimensional characters, you'll want to start with the basics and branch out from there. To see how this might work, say your main character is a woman in her early twenties. Here are some of the facts you may start with:

Name: Jessica Kane

Age: Twenty-five

Occupation: Journalist

Place of Birth: Brooklyn, NY

With these dry, external basics, we can begin to develop our blueprint for Jessica.

Let's start with her age. As a twenty-five-year-old, her worldview is going to be very different from a forty-year-old or even an eighteen-year-old. She's been through college and started a career—so she's probably savvier than someone who's still going to school. (Let's hope!) However, she doesn't have enough experience to see things the way a forty-year-old would. She might be a little less entrenched in her worldview, maybe a little more forgiving. Or maybe she's hardheaded and critical, thus, more judgmental because of her lack of living experience.

Now, let's move on to her place of birth and economic status. As I discussed earlier, where and how she is raised is probably the most important contributor to a character's lens. Did your character grow up in a leafy suburb with high-achieving professionals in well-tended upscale homes, or in a fifth-floor walk-up in a depressed urban environment where danger is part of the scenery?

Or perhaps your character grew up on a struggling farm or was the child of diplomats and lived all over the world in privileged settings. The more specific you are in creating your character's history, the sharper drawn your character will be—and the more enjoyment your readers will have.

Let's return to Jessica and see how we can start to build a Character Blueprint for her:

Place of Birth: Brooklyn, NY

Economic Status: Family was poor; grew up in the Projects.

Parents' Key Phrase: "Work hard, pay your bills, don't make waves, and you'll get along fine in life."

Character Lens: "Playing by the rules is for suckers. If you want to get anywhere in life you have to break the rules— or make your own."

These facts will help you to begin to determine just what it is your character *needs*, which will be a key motivator in his or her actions throughout the novel. For instance, as a journalist, Jessica might be drawn to investigative journalism because she *needs* to find cracks in the system that held her family—and her—down. She *needs* to expose injustice to help overcome her past as a victim. She might take huge risks to get her story, going against her boss's directives, perhaps even putting her own life in danger. She views her job much differently than her boss. She's a crusader; he's a news gatherer.

OPENING WINDOWS INTO YOUR CHARACTER

Years ago I took a writing workshop that had participants come up with a lengthy list of traits for their main characters. We couldn't stop until we reached fifty traits. I diligently did my homework, stretching all credulity to come up with a hodge-podge list. I thought I came up with some really clever traits. Trouble was, they were really just a laundry list of tics and habits, likes and dislikes. But they didn't add up to a vivid picture of my characters. That's because I didn't know my characters' histories—where they came from or what factors in the past made them who they were in the present. Therefore, the traits didn't offer windows into the characters' true selves.

So, how do we get from "trait" to "window?" Let's return to Jessica the journalist and start with a basic set of traits you might give her:

- Tough-talking

- Loves animals

- Exercise nut

- Smarter than most people around her

- Kind to old people

- Impatient with people she perceives as incompetent

- Can't resist dessert

- Loves to tell jokes

- Pretty blonde

Sounds like a dossier, doesn't it? And it's about as interesting as one, too. To transform this list of traits into windows, we need to go back to the history you created for Jessica. Since she grew up in the projects, these traits are going to manifest in very different ways than if she grew up a child of privilege. Let's take each trait and apply it as it would pertain to each of these circumstances. The box on the following page shows us two possible blueprints for Jessica.

CHARACTER BLUEPRINT:
JESSICA

	(Blueprint A)	(Blueprint B)
	Grew up in the projects	Child of privilege
Tough-talking:	Comes by it naturally. That's how you survived.	Developed it as a way to distinguish herself from the other "richies."
Loves animals:	Sees animals as sources of comfort. Identifies with strays—they don't ask favors.	Pets are meant to be pampered. An animal must be pedigreed.
Exercise nut:	Runs. That's what she did as a kid. Who could afford a gym?	Pilates. Has a personal trainer. To let oneself go is a sign of weakness.
Smarter:	Had to be to survive. Her "smarts" are street smarts— she understands people and knows how to get what she needs.	Thanks to all that private tutoring!
Kind to old people:	What would her grandmother say if she weren't?	A person of good breeding is kind to those in need.
Impatient with incompetence:	"I worked my ass off to get where I am, so where do you come off being so lazy?"	"There are right and wrong ways of doing things." Protocol and procedures must be followed.
Loves dessert:	Oreo cookies.	Crème brûlée.
Jokes:	Good, bad, dirty, or corny— jokes are good for winning over people and getting them to do what you want.	Dumb blonde jokes. It's a way of letting others know that she doesn't take herself too seriously.
Pretty blonde:	Feels out of place, like a splash of bleach on a lovely, dark sweater.	A three-color process that Mother Nature would envy.
Needs:	To find cracks in the system that held her family—and her— down. To expose injustice to help overcome her past as a victim.	To prove that she has the mettle to be a crack journalist. To change the system so that it's fair to rich and poor alike.

BEFORE MOVING ON

1. Determine your main character's history. Do the same for all the major players.
2. Come up with a list of traits you'd like to give your characters.
3. Transform those traits into windows by tying them to your characters' histories.
4. Create a Character Blueprint for each character and post them where you can see them. (We'll be using them in the next chapter.) You may even want to find a photo of a model or actor who resembles your character and attach that to the blueprint.

Give yourself plenty of time to allow this process to unfold. Don't be afraid to discard ideas in favor of other ones—no matter how off-the-wall they may seem. Often, the first idea that comes to mind is not always the most interesting for your characters. Observe real people in life and ask yourself what their "blueprint" might be. In the next chapter, we'll be diving into the deep with your characters, getting to know them even better.

3

JOURNEY TO THE CENTER OF YOUR CHARACTERS

Get to Know Your Cast Better Than Yourself

BY NOW, YOU should have Character Blueprints drawn up for all the major members of your cast. But there's still a bit more to it. The most memorable stories have characters who transcend the limits of the physical page. They are the ones who linger in your mind, even when the book is closed—someone you could bump into on the street and feel you know well enough to stop and say hello to (or to run quickly away from, as the case may be). This kind of intimacy comes from one thing, and one thing alone: journeying to the center of your characters, and figuring out what, exactly, is at the core of their particular personas.

"SHRINKING" YOUR CHARACTERS

If you want to make your characters really big and really compelling, you're going to need to shrink them—meaning, put them on the therapist's couch and begin asking them about their deepest, darkest secrets. Shrinking your characters is great for you plotters, because it will push you to think of them beyond their function in playing out your story's plot. For pantsers, too, shrinking your characters will make you pause and develop a more dimensional portrait than you'd ever likely create by writing on the fly. So, what would you ask your character to try to get to know her better, to find out what *really* makes her tick? Here are some questions to help get you started:

What is his biggest strength?

Another way of asking this question: What is your character better at or smarter in than anybody else? This question allows you to create characters who can serve the needs of your plot, as well as characters who the reader will admire. This question also allows you to use characters to convey important information, as well as to provide much-needed tension and conflict.

What is her biggest weakness?

One of my authors was writing a novel whose main character was a special ops officer. The character was likeable, and smart, and had many strengths. But he wasn't particularly interesting because he had no vulnerabilities. The author was afraid to give his character any weaknesses because he feared that the character would lose his heroic qualities. But it was just the opposite. What makes a true hero is someone who has weaknesses and is able to overcome them for the greater good. Once this author was able to give his character a weakness, the scenes had more tension and the character actually became much more likeable. Let's face it: we all have weaknesses. When we read about other characters—even those much smarter or braver or more talented than we are—we feel better about ourselves if the characters have some weakness to overcome.

What past mistake does he regret?

The past always informs the present. And a character who regrets something she did in the past will try to right it somehow in the present of your story. By giving your character a mistake in the past, you provide her with an internal motivation for her actions.

What was her biggest dream or goal in life?

What did your character want to be before your story started? An artist? A doctor? A high-ranking politician? Did he want to change the world? Or live a quiet life in the woods?

How does that dream contrast with the reality she now finds herself in?

Think of the character who wanted to become a crusading lawyer only to find that the actual practice of law is stultifying. Or the girl who dreamed of becoming an actress only to find herself waiting tables? These contrasts make for great conflict and inner tension.

What does he love most or hate most about his work?

Asking questions that demand the opposite can help infuse your scenes with a richness, as well as create more conflict. For instance, an ER doctor might love the adrenaline rush that comes from saving a patient from death, but hate having to inform the family when he loses a patient. A school teacher might love imparting the lessons to his students, but despise dealing with the administration.

What are her rituals?

Rituals offer great clues to characters and can enrich your scenes with great texture. A ritual can be as simple as a lawyer lining up her pad and pencil neatly on the table and then buttoning her jacket before giving her final summation, or as complex as the rituals of a serial killer. Think of *Darkly Dreaming Dexter* by Jeff Lindsay. Dexter is an "avenging angel," a serial killer who targets other serial killers who have evaded the law. Before he plunges the foot-long blade into his victims, he first slices their cheeks and collects a sample of blood on a slide, to be stored in a box with the slides of other victims. This ritual not only fits in with Dexter's day job of being a blood splatter analyst for the Miami Metro Police, but it serves as a souvenir of the act.

What are his quirks?

Is your character repulsed by brussels sprouts? Is he compelled to straighten pictures on the walls? Does she twist her ring before telling a lie? Characters are often not aware of their own quirks, but the quirks can be great fodder for other characters to respond to.

What personality trait gets her into trouble?

Does your character have a tendency to tell the truth, even when it could work against her? Does he automatically say "black" when others say "white?" Does she take in stray animals? Does he jump in and help others—even when they don't want help?

What does she know "for sure?"

I call this the "Oprah question." This gets at the core being of your character, the one thing she knows either about herself, or human nature, or the workings of the world, that drives her to act the way she does. For instance, say your character knows "for sure" that deep down, all people are good. That belief may end up putting her in jeopardy—or result in her not giving up on a child who others have written off as "bad to the core."

What doesn't he know about himself?

A character may not know how prejudiced she is, or how capable she is in a crisis. He may not know that he has a natural gift for healing others, or that he sabotages relationships before they even get going. This question provides some great fodder for story events or turning points.

What is she hiding?

It takes tremendous energy to hide elements of ourselves or facts about our past, which in turn creates inner turmoil. What fun for the writer! Say your novel is set in the South prior to the Civil Rights Act, and say your character is of mixed race but has been able to "pass" as White. Or suppose your character committed a heinous crime when he was a teenager that went unsolved? By giving your character something to hide, you force her to confront this secret later on in the story.

What is the one thing he fears most?

Does he fear abandonment? Poverty? Fire? Parenthood? Again, asking a question like this will make you thrust your character into situations that force him to confront his fear.

What would she never do?

This is one of my favorite questions because it's a setup for a big "Moment of Truth" for your character (*we'll discuss this in more depth in the next chapter*). For instance, let's say your main character is the CEO of a previously successful company that employs thousands of workers. He has always vowed that he would never offshore his manufacturing—no matter what. But now he is faced with either offshoring his manufacturing or losing his entire company, which means the thousands of workers who depend on their jobs would be out of work. What does he do?

Do you have a character who's an investigative reporter who has vowed never to sleep with a source to get a piece of information? Well then, you know what you're going to have to do sometime in the course of the story: make it so that she has no choice but to sleep with a source to get her information because to not do so would have far greater ramifications.

What does he need?

This is the über question of sorts. All of the previous questions are leading you to come up with the larger "need" of your character. And it's this need that informs every action she takes—or doesn't take.

Answering these questions for each of your characters is going to take some time. But this is time very well spent at this stage of the novel-writing process. When you know your characters almost better than you know yourself, they will practically write the story for you.

GOING BEYOND THE MUG SHOT

Once you fully understand your characters on the inside, you'll be able to construct them physically on the outside. It's the outer wrappings that truly reflect what is on the inside. Too often, I've seen writers come up with character descriptions that—while incredibly detailed—actually tell us nothing about the character. Instead, what we have is a "mug shot" of sorts that tells us a character's height, age, weight, hair and eye color, etc. But we don't get a picture of that character; we're not shown the character in a way that the reader can really envision.

Imagine your protagonist is an insecure teenaged boy. How can you describe him without once stating any of these descriptors ("insecure" or "teenaged") directly? Here's how one writer did it:

> He was growing into his nose, slowly. Each week his eyes seemed to settle a little deeper on either side of it, pushing his brow out like an awning over his roundish face. His mouth, usually shut in a shy, flat line, was increasingly agape, awed by the world, and flashed his teeth, which were belted into his gums by unfortunate blue braces. At night, they attached to a formidable cage of metal headgear that, only once at a sleepover, had he allowed his best friend to see.
>
> —BRIANNA FLAHERTY

Here, the boy's facial features convey much more than just his physicality. We don't need to be directly told that he is an insecure, slightly awkward boy—the author implies these details by noting that he's still growing into some of his features, and still a bit shy. Pay particular attention to the description of the boy's mouth. It reveals simultaneously that the character is maturing (his mouth is "increasingly agape, awed by the world"), and that he still harbors youthful insecurities, such as his reluctance to let anyone see him in his headgear. We are given a clear image of an adolescent boy, anxious about his appearance and eager to transition into the seeming security of adulthood—an experience many readers can relate to.

Even minor characters should get their due. Too often, beginning writers fail to pay attention to the walk-ons. And that's a mistake. When you describe a minor character generically, the scene doesn't come as alive as it should. Worse—crucial details may be lost because the reader's eyes just glazed over that part. You don't have to do much to cement a minor character's image in the reader's mind. Take a look at this passage, from Tom Farrell's *The Kelso Club*:

> About forty-five minutes later I got a knock on my door. A guy in a musty, mud-colored overcoat with a face that reminded me of a grouper fish stared back at me.

What reader will forget that character when he's mentioned in passing later on in the story?

So, now you can see how a person's worldview can take a set of generic traits and turn them into specific character traits. You know a little bit more about what makes your character tick. You understand where your character "is coming from." You have found specific details with which to paint your character descriptions. When you do this, you will end up with a character who's more flesh-and-blood—and interesting to your readers!

But your job is not over just yet. You need to do this work for every major character in your book. Eventually, you should find that the work becomes fun—as you begin to develop their blueprints and fall in love with your characters, your readers will, too.

BEFORE MOVING ON

Be sure to "shrink" all of your major characters. Don't be afraid to come up with your own questions, especially those that may be particular to your story. If you find yourself stuck, with any one character, see how you can come up with answers that may be in juxtaposition to your main character. And don't be afraid to go out on a limb with "crazy" answers! You can always dial it back, but it might offer you some creative possibilities that you hadn't thought of before.

AUTHOR INSIGHT

While writing my thriller novel, *Smokescreen*, I wondered if it would be possible to develop an out-of-body experience for writing my characters—to let each and every one of them take over my mind. The answer lies in method writing.

To make the characters come alive, I allowed myself to become lost inside each character's head. In the process, I had to shed my identity and transform into every character to understand each individual better.

As a writer, you can choreograph a scene to know what it feels like to be in that atmosphere. You can play pretend by using the power of imagination and letting the character create the scene—not you.

What a writer can also do is to study people's behavior in everyday life. It doesn't matter where you are; whether you're sitting at a café or riding a bus, you can observe all aspects of behavior—from facial expressions, body language, tone of voice, diction to clothing.

For me, I enjoy conducting an imaginary séance before I work on my manuscripts. I allow the sensation of writing to spiritually conjure the characters, after which I become "possessed" as I work on different pages and chapters. By channeling the different characters into my mind, I begin to feel, to be, and to do.

Method writing is also useful in handling dialogues. You may write a voice well, but will it sound good if spoken out loud? To put this to a test, imagine speaking in an angry tone or being drunk. The dialogue must not sound awkward, so best to act it out.

You can also use this technique to pull yourself into parallel worlds and enter other dimensions. Whatever and whoever you choose to be—a human, an alien or a ghost—it's not strange to be a method writer with a little bit of imagination. But do remember to self-exorcise yourself at the end of the day to become you again.

—Khaled Talib, author of *Smokescreen*

INTERVIEWING YOUR CHARACTERS

Ask these questions of your characters to get to know them on a deeper level:

What is his biggest strength?

What is her biggest weakness?

What past mistake does he regret?

What was her biggest dream or goal in life?

How does that dream contrast with the reality she now finds herself in?

What does he love most or hate most about his work?

What are her rituals?

What are his quirks?

What personality trait gets her into trouble?

What does she know "for sure?"

What doesn't he know about himself?

What is she hiding?

What is the one thing he fears most?

What would she never do?

What does he need?

4

THE STORY FRAMEWORK

Establishing the Key Moments

BY NOW YOU should have a pretty good idea of who and what your novel is going to be about. You've delved deep into your characters, and you have a pretty good idea of what makes them tick. You know what kind of story you want to tell and what ideas and themes you are exploring. But how do you take all this information and put it into a story? Too often, I've seen writers just dive in and start writing scenes. *After all*, they think, *I've done the hard work of figuring out my characters. Shouldn't I just let them loose on the page and see where they take me?* This is not necessarily a good idea.

Why? Because you can't trust your characters. You heard that right: you can't trust your characters to tell the story. This may seem a bit counterintuitive. I'm sure you've heard many successful authors say, "My characters seemed to have lives of their own. I didn't write that story. I just got out of the way and let my characters tell *their* story." What the successful author doesn't say, however, is that by now in his writing career, he has an almost intuitive sense of story structure. Over the years, that writer has found an instinctual balance between plotting and pantsing when he approaches story structure—the rest of us, especially first-time authors, don't always have this intuitive luxury.

Think of your characters as toddlers: you wouldn't just let a two-year-old loose in a toy store and say, "You pick out whatever you like, darling." You will either end up with a shopping cart overflowing with pretty much every single item in the store, or your toddler will have a meltdown when faced with the prospect of all those choices. Likewise, if you just let your characters loose on the page, you can either end up with a story going off in all sorts of tangents leading to nowhere, or you might write yourself into a corner and give up in frustration.

Providing a structure for your characters will allow them to unfold in a way that serves the story.

Understanding story structure will give you a clear idea of where you're headed and how to get there. Providing a structure for your characters will allow them to unfold in a way that serves the story. Notice I didn't say "serves the plot." You are not a puppet master forcing wooden characters to do things you want them to do because you have a preconceived idea of what you want to happen. That's why we started with character first. Certainly, coming up with a story structure now doesn't mean it's etched in stone. It's your prerogative to change your mind as you go along. Perhaps your characters, indeed, may lead you to a better alternative. But for now—when you're at the beginning stages of planning out your novel—you need to provide your characters with a solid foundation upon which to act.

Just as you created a Character Blueprint in the last lesson, you need to create a Story Framework—the Key Moments you need to hit in your novel. I'm not talking *formula*, but rather a way to move the story along in an interesting way that ratchets up the suspense and keeps the reader wanting to find out what happens. If you've ever read a novel that didn't quite grab you, despite great characters and an interesting plot, chances are it was the structure that was off.

This chapter will help you build a solid Story Framework that will not only make the writing go much easier, but will ultimately result in a satisfying story for your reader.

UNDERSTANDING STORY STRUCTURE

Ultimately, the structure is where plot and character journey converge. That's why we developed the Character Blueprint first—you cannot create the structure without first understanding your main character and what he or she wants.

While all novels are made up of countless scenes and turning points, there are **six Key Moments** you need to have in place first before you start writing everything else. These six moments form the foundation of your novel. Everything else that happens revolves in some way around these Key Moments. Let me first lay these out for you, and then I'll explain each moment so you understand what they need to accomplish and how to create them:

STORY FRAMEWORK

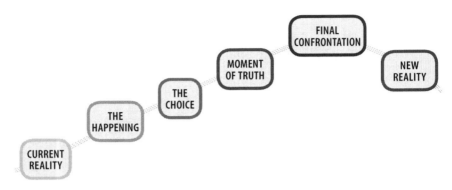

These boxes each represent the six Key Moments in the novel that must happen for the story to be complete. Let's take a look at each of these moments.

CURRENT REALITY

This is not a moment, per se, but rather the establishment of your main character and the setting. We see how he is in his everyday life, how he interacts with the world. This usually takes up a very small portion of the novel—just enough to make your reader enter the world you've created and care about your main character. You are creating a world according to *this* story—whether it's a realistic story set in Maine in the current day, a historical drama set in India during the time of British rule, or a fantasy world of your own creation.

The Current Reality is not, however, an exploration of back-story—everything that happened to your character *before* the story got started. Too often, one of the biggest mistakes I see first-time authors making is that they front-load their novels with history in the mistaken belief that readers need to know everything about the characters in order to be fully invested in them. Remember all that work you did in the last chapter developing your characters fully and knowing their histories? Guess what? That's all eventually going to come into play during the course of your story—just not all in the beginning. (*For more on how and when to use backstory, go to Chapter 11.*)

The Current Reality is not an exploration of backstory—but of what is happening in your character's life right now.

Instead, the Current Reality is what is happening in your character's life *right now*. What are the circumstances of his life if everything was to keep on going the way it has?

Is your character a dedicated ER doctor, working punishing hours in an understaffed hospital to save the lives of his patients? Then show him saving a patient's life, despite the lack of enough nurses to help in the process. Show his exhaustion and exasperation. That's his Current Reality.

Is your character a burned-out news reporter? Then show her gathering news on yet another robbery that resulted in a shooting. Show her attitude about doing this kind of story. If she's burned out, show her missing crucial details because of her jadedness. Show her getting reamed out by her editor for sloppy reporting. Show her going home to an empty apartment and dining on ramen noodles. That's her Current Reality.

Let's say your main character is a suburban wife and mother with two children. To the outside observer, her life seems idyllic, but she harbors resentment toward her family, believing she's missing out on something more exciting. Each day her routine is the same: get the kids up, feed everyone breakfast, drop her husband off at the train station, then drop the kids off at school, take a Zumba class, go home. This is her Current Reality. And you're going to show those activities—and how she feels about them— in the opening pages of your novel. Notice I said "pages" and not "chapters." The Current Reality should be dealt with swiftly. This is a way to let readers meet your main character, get to know her a little bit, and get a glimpse of her life before the s**t hits the fan. That's all.

If you're writing sci-fi, fantasy, or historical drama, then show your character's Current Reality through a few telling details that ground the reader in the time, place, and characteristics of your novel. Avoid the temptation to spend pages and pages on setting up the world. (*For more on how to incorporate research into your novel, read Chapter 11.*)

Sure, developing a rich backstory is critical—I'd be willing to bet that the map included at the start of *The Hobbit* was initially made so J. R. R. Tolkien could lay out a clear picture for himself of the vast world he envisioned. But as impressive as Tolkien's fantasy world is, there would hardly be space in the novel for Bilbo Baggins to journey through Middle Earth if the author described every inch of his story's landscape and history in the actual text. Instead, Tolkien delivers a direct, vivid picture of Bilbo's Current Reality.

Bilbo's home, for example, is referred to as The Hill—a sheltered, warm, isolated space in a world that seems so small, it could only contain one literal hill. The reader gets a snapshot, then, of Bilbo's simple, small-town life, without having to wade through pages and pages of backstory. If Tolkien spent several chapters setting up the world of Middle Earth, it's unlikely that his novel would be the gripping fantasy tale we've come to know.

THE HAPPENING

Shortly after we're introduced to the main character and his world, some disturbance has to happen to shake up that world. Think of a placid pond as the Current Reality. Now, picture what happens when a stone is cast into that pond. The water is disturbed and ripples form. Likewise, the Happening sets up the problem of the story and puts the plot in motion.

Let's take a look at the examples mentioned earlier to see how this might unfold.

Dedicated, but stressed, ER doctor: One day he saves the life of a woman who is running from the drug cartel who have forced her into being a drug mule. She begs him to help her.

Burned-out reporter: One day, while reporting what seems like a routine story, she comes across information that could result in bringing down a powerful politician.

Disillusioned suburban mom: One day after she arrives home from her Zumba class, an old boyfriend—the one true love of her life—shows up at her door.

Each of these events is the Happening—the stone cast upon the pond. In each of these Happenings, the story problem and the main character's central question is implied:

Will the doctor help the drug mule escape, knowing he could be risking his own life?

Will the reporter choose to pursue the story about the corrupt politician, knowing she could put her career as a reporter in jeopardy?

Will the mom choose her ex-boyfriend over her family, knowing the damage she would inflict on her husband and children?

THE CHOICE

This is the moment when the main character makes a decision—or has a decision thrust upon her—that will forever alter the course of events. Once this character crosses the threshold, things can never go back to the way they were before. Now, your character may make a series of choices that lead up to the one big Choice. This big choice is the one that makes it a Key Moment. Here's what I mean:

Getting back to our suburban mom example, the Choice may be that she decides to run off with her ex-lover, leaving behind her predictable life in favor of the thrill of danger and the promise of the passion that's so lacking in her current life. But most likely, she didn't just come to that choice after Mr. Perfect-in-the-Past showed up at her door. She had to make a whole bunch of little choices: to let him inside, to meet with him on the sly, to lie to her husband and kids. Those are all smaller choices that lead up to the Key Moment of the Choice of leaving her family.

MOMENT OF TRUTH

This is the biggest turning point for your character. It is the moment that everything else has been leading toward, the point at which your main character will either rise above her problem or sink into it. It is also the moment that sets up the final confrontation. This is the most important scene in your novel, the scene that encapsulates the novel's problem and the main character's central question.

Getting back to our suburban mom, her Moment of Truth could be a scene in which she sees her ex-lover for the low-life he really is—and sees the damage she has caused her family because of her selfishness.

FINAL CONFRONTATION

Sometimes this scene comes nearly simultaneous to the Moment of Truth. If not, it's very close on its heels. This is where the character battles it out with his opponent, where his Moment of Truth is put to the test. Even though it's called the Final Confrontation, that doesn't necessarily mean big things have to happen. It could be as quiet as a high-flying executive getting up and walking out of a shareholder's meeting. In our suburban mom example, it could be as flashy as an actual knock-down, drag-out fight to the finish with the ex-lover, or as quiet as her secretly calling the authorities and turning him in.

NEW REALITY

You have put your character to the test: she has confronted her demons, she has forever changed, she has proven herself in the ultimate test. And now she finds herself in a New Reality—a vastly changed state from the Current Reality at the beginning of the novel. This is where you give the reader satisfaction—a feeling of resonance—and where all the loose ends are tied up. For instance, the suburban mom has come to realize the important role she has in her husband's and children's lives and returns home. But she has done serious damage to her marriage and her relationship with her children. There's hope for a new beginning, and that is because the main character has changed.

STORY STRUCTURE IN *THE GODFATHER*

Let's now take a look at an actual story to see how this structure plays out. I've chosen Francis Ford Coppola's filmed version of Mario Puzo's *The Godfather* because the structure is very clear and because it's a story that most people are familiar with. Or if you're not familiar with it, you can easily rent the film. One caveat: This structure follows the movie version of *The Godfather, Part I,* which roughly corresponds to the first third of Puzo's enormous saga. Each subsequent film (and subsequent part of the novel) has its own structure.

Current Reality: Young Michael Corleone, a war hero, is home from the war. While at a family gathering, he assures his innocent fiancé that he is determined to lead a law-abiding life and avoid his father's way of life as a Mafia Don. This sets up the problem and the central question: will Michael be able to avoid being pulled into a life of crime?

The Happening: Michael's father, Don Corleone, is shot by an adversary and nearly killed. This is the ripple in Michael's world. He may choose to act or not.

The Choice: After getting his jaw broken by the crooked police chief (who is on the payroll of his father's adversary), Michael vows revenge on the rival family and masterminds their murder, committing the act himself. By committing this act of murder, Michael can never go back to his earlier way of life. He has now been pulled into the Mafia.

Moment of Truth: Michael sets in motion a plot to decimate the rival families, which will establish him as the new Don of the Corleone family. Michael has thoroughly sunk into that which he at first repelled: a life of crime. His dark side is released and there is no turning back.

Final Confrontation: While Michael and his family are in the midst of a baptism, his soldiers carry out the plan, unleashing a torrent of death upon the family's enemies.

New Reality: Confronted by his wife, who asks if he was responsible for the death of his brother-in-law Carlo, Michael boldly lies and denies it. He has gone from being an idealistic, law-abiding war hero at the beginning of the story to being the kingpin of the thoroughly corrupt family business.

Certainly the story is far more complex than I've made it here. The important thing to note is that each of these Key Moments ratchets up the stakes, making for a suspenseful, emotionally wrenching story.

Why is it so important to know your story's Key Moments before you start writing?

Because once you know these points, every scene you write is either leading up to the turning point or leading away from it. This helps you build tension as you approach the moment, and then release it outward in ever-widening ripples of impact.

BEFORE MOVING ON

Create your Story Framework. For each Key Moment, write a sentence or two that describes what takes place and how that plays into the moment. Aim to keep this to one page in length. Remember: These are moments—not entire sequences.

AUTHOR INSIGHT

I had written several nonfiction books, but this was my first attempt at a novel. Following Diane's practical and extremely sage advice, I have been able to convert my opening text, which had been more of an "info dump," into something that allows the story to unfold by showing my main character's Current Reality and how she behaves in her "ordinary life."

I originally didn't think this approach would be too exciting, but Diane showed me how to take the reader immediately into the world I wanted to create and set the stage for a key development in the next chapter.

Now that readers know what my main character is all about, they can better follow the impact of changes and begin to appreciate her journey.

—Carolyn Kay Brancato, author of *Night of the Maquis*

KEY MOMENTS

Current Reality: What is happening in your character's life right now. (Note: Do not get bogged down in backstory.)

The Happening: The disturbance that shakes up your character's world.

The Choice: The main character makes a decision that will forever alter the course of events. (Note: You can have a series of choices leading up to one big Choice.)

Moment of Truth: The biggest turning point for your character; the scene that encapsulates the novel's problem and the main character's central question.

Final Confrontation: The Moment of Truth is put to the test; the main character battles it out with her opponent.

New Reality: The world as it has changed for your main character. (Note: This better be a BIG change!)

5

FOCUSING THE LENS
Choosing Point of View

I N MY EXPERIENCE working with authors and in the classes I've taught, point of view (POV) is the one area that befuddles most first-time authors. This chapter will, hopefully, clear up some misconceptions and help give you the foundation for making a choice that serves your story and your characters.

When I talk about POV, what I mean is, which character is going to be the conduit through which the reader experiences the story? Will it be told through your main character's eyes only, or through the lens of multiple characters? Will you be writing in first person POV, third person limited, multiple POV, or some other, less-used POV, such as omniscient? While some authors know immediately when they first get an idea how they will handle POV, others may not be immediately clear which way to go at this stage of the game.

But now is precisely the right time to make these choices— before you spend too much time committed to a POV that is not serving the story well. All too often, pantsers will start off writing in a particular POV because that's what comes most naturally. Plotters, on the other hand, often find themselves committed to a particular POV because they hadn't thought of any other possibility. Writers in both the plotter and pantser camps run the risk, then, of getting to the end of their draft, after spending months or even years of working on it, only to find out that the POV they chose was not the most effective one.

The time to choose POV is before you start writing your manuscript.

The time to choose POV is *before* you start writing your manuscript. While that may sound pretty obvious, there are a lot of variables you need to consider before making your decision.

For example, let's say you want to write your novel in the first person. The protagonist may not necessarily be the most effective POV character. *The Great Gatsby* for instance, is about Jay Gatsby, but he's not the one telling the story. The novel is told from the POV of Nick Carraway, the visiting cousin of Daisy Buchanan— Gatsby's true love, who happens to be married to Tom Buchanan.

Nick is an outsider and so has no immediate stake in what happens to Gatsby or even Daisy, whom he barely knows. But it's precisely this status that allows Nick to tell the story most objectively. As the outsider, Nick gives the reader a privy look at the idle rich. He reveals their flippant carelessness and lack of regard for those beneath them. His point of view leads the reader to conclude, as he does, that these characters are drifters, floating through lives bereft of moral meaning. The closer he gets to them, the shallower they become, finally leaving him feeling tainted and repulsed by their sins. Nick is able to offer an insight that no other character could have. Because of this, the novel has so much more breadth and depth than it would have if it had been told through either Gatsby's or Daisy's POV—or even multiple POVs.

In Harper Lee's *To Kill a Mockingbird*, the story is told through Scout, the nine-year-old daughter of Atticus Finch. Any one of the principal characters in this classic novel could have been a POV character: the small-town lawyer, Atticus; the accused, Tom Robinson; the woman who accused him of raping her, Mayella Ewell. However, by telling the story from the POV of an innocent child, Harper Lee is able to give greater impact to the message of this timeless novel: the lesson of tolerance and the courage it takes to stand up for the truth. In the beginning of the story, Atticus tells Scout that there are "many different viewpoints in the world," and that she should never judge anyone else's ideas until she has looked at them from that person's point of view.

So, where do you start? How do you know what the best POV approach is for your novel? Before you lock yourself in, it helps to know how each of the choices work, including the strengths and weaknesses of each approach. Keep in mind, there's no one right answer, and you may even want to experiment a bit with each before settling on your POV approach. The key is to have a firm understanding of each before diving in and writing an entire manuscript with the wrong approach!

FIRST PERSON

When a story is told from the point of view of "I" it is referred to as first person. This POV often seems like the most natural one to write in for novice authors. It's easy to see why. There are many advantages to writing in the first person.

Advantages

It allows you to fully explore a character's journey and thought processes. When you're only inside one character's head, it becomes easier to develop that character.

You create an emotional bond with your reader. Because all the protagonist's thoughts and feelings can be revealed, readers feel like they "know" the character. More so than any other POV, first person creates a greater sense of intimacy between the character and the reader. Remember reading *The Catcher in the Rye* in high school? What teenager didn't feel as though Holden Caulfield was speaking directly to him or her?

You can get inside the character's head in a more vivid way than with third person. The transitions from exterior narrative and dialogue to interior thoughts can be a lot easier to accomplish because there is no separation between the narrator and the POV character.

You can create empathy for a potentially disagreeable character. If your main character is a killer or a busybody neighbor, you really want to have the reader be inside that character's head to know why they act the way they do. Remember the Dexter Morgan novels we talked about in the previous chapter? By telling the stories from Dexter Morgan's POV in the first person, author Jeff Lindsay actually gives the reader a real sense of what makes this serial killer tick. We feel like we know him intimately, and so we give ourselves over to the ride.

With mysteries, first person POV can give readers the chance to solve the crime along with the sleuth. This may be the biggest advantage for mystery writers—if that's the effect you're going for.

You can establish a distinct, original voice for your narrator. Because the POV character and the narrator are one and the same, this allows you the opportunity for infusing humor, sarcasm, teenage-speak, etc., into the narration, whereas if you were writing in the third person, this would seem like author intrusion.

Drawbacks

You are limited to what your character sees, hears, feels, and thinks. And that can come to feel like a straightjacket. Once you are in your protagonist's head, you're stuck there. You can't have your character commenting on a conversation that's occurring out of her earshot, you can't have her describing what someone is doing unless she actually sees them, and you can't ever tell us what another character is thinking or feeling.

You can only write scenes in which your character is present. That means you can't have a scene in which the POV character's boyfriend is cheating on her—unless she happens to witness it.

There's a danger that your character is not interesting enough for an entire book. What's more interesting? Taking a cross-country road trip with someone who obeys all the traffic laws, knows exactly where he's going, doesn't have any bad habits, is agreeable and even-tempered, and listens to elevator music? Or taking a road trip with a person who thinks speed limits are for sissies, nurses a bottle of whiskey while driving, has an arsenal the size of Utah in his trunk, flips off anyone who cuts him off in traffic, and can spin a spellbinding tale that makes you cringe and laugh and sit on the edge of your seat wanting to know what happened next? The rational person would choose driver #1, but if you're out for adventure—and all readers are, if only in their imaginations—you'll go with driver #2.

WHEN CONSIDERING FIRST PERSON, ASK YOURSELF:

Does this character have a distinctive, colorful voice? People want to read about characters who have a different take on the world than they do—that's what makes great characters stick in the mind long after the story has ended. If your character does not offer a fresh view on events and the people around him, then why would readers want to see the world from his POV?

Will this character be everywhere I need him to be and know everything I need him to know? This is really crucial and needs to be answered *before* you start writing. You do not want to get to page 150 and find that a critical scene must take place that your POV character cannot possibly be present for.

Do I want readers to identify strongly with this character? It doesn't matter if your POV character is a serial killer, a beat cop, a nerdy teen, a rock musician, or an astrophysicist. There must be something about that person that readers will recognize in themselves.

Do I want to spend several hundred pages—and hundreds of hours—inside this character's head? You've got to really love this character because she will come to dominate your own thoughts. If you find out halfway through writing your manuscript that you really don't like this character—or worse, are bored by her—you'll never be able to complete your book.

Examples of Bestsellers That Use First Person

In the Woods by Tana French

Lolita by Vladimir Nabokov

Twilight by Stephenie Meyer

The Handmaid's Tale by Margaret Atwood

Ready Player One by Ernest Cline

The House on Mango Street by Sandra Cisneros

The Adventures of Huckleberry Finn by Mark Twain

THIRD PERSON LIMITED

Just as with first person POV, third person limited tells the story through the eyes of only one character. The most obvious difference is that instead of having the narrator of the story be one and the same, you have stepped a bit outside of the POV character and are telling it through a different narrator. So, instead of the character referring to him or herself as "I," you have your narrator referring to the POV character as "he" or "she."

Why would you want to do this? Well, third person limited allows you to tell your story from the viewpoint of only one character, but you do have a bit more flexibility in how you approach your story. Let's take a look at the advantages that writing in third person limited has over first person.

Advantages

You can show things the character doesn't see. You don't have to worry about "eyes in the back of the head."

You have more freedom with description. By stepping out of your character's head, you can describe things with more depth than your character may be able to.

You can be more objective. This is helpful when you've got a POV character who may not always be reliable.

You don't have to spend so much time inside a character's head. This can combat the feeling of claustrophobia, giving your readers a break from seeing everything through the lens of your character.

Drawbacks

There's a danger of seeming removed. You don't want to leave a reader wondering why you didn't just write this in first person POV.

The story can feel a bit flat. Because you are a bit more removed from the main character, the internal conflict may not be as apparent. Your main character's journey can become obscured by the larger plot, leaving the reader feeling detached from the emotional core of the story.

There's the temptation of author intrusion. Clichéd examples of author intrusion are phrases such as "little did he know that ...," or, "he wouldn't realize the significance of finding the empty beer bottle on the front steps until much later."

WHEN CONSIDERING THIRD PERSON LIMITED, ASK YOURSELF:

Are readers going to be as invested in the story as I want them to be? Remember: Writing in the third person is slightly more removed from the character. It's not as up close and personal as first person.

Am I more comfortable writing in the third person? You might also believe your readers will be more comfortable with your character if written in the third person (for instance, if she's not a sympathetic character, if she suffers from mental illness, or if she's just plain weird). This gives the character room to be honest, while allowing readers to stay with him without feeling contaminated by the character.

Do I want to increase the emotional distance from the character? If your main character is a killer, for instance, you may *not* want to be entirely in his head for the novel. Limited third person allows you to stay with this one character throughout without creating too much of an emotional involvement on the part of your readers. Ask if you want your readers to struggle with the moral implications of feeling sympathy for a murderer.

Would my story be better served if I wrote it in the first person? If you're not sure, try writing a portion of your story in both first person and limited third to help you answer this question.

Examples of Bestsellers That Use Third Person Limited

For Whom the Bell Tolls by Ernest Hemingway

The Call of the Wild by Jack London

An Unexpected Grace by Kristin von Kreisler

THIRD PERSON MULTIPLE

In third person multiple, you have a number of key POV characters who you choose to tell your story. There are a lot of advantages to writing in third person multiple.

Advantages

It allows for much more complexity. Little by little, readers begin to get all sides of the story, which allows them to emotionally invest themselves in a number of characters. They find themselves rooting for some to succeed and others to fail. They may be surprised when they become aligned with an "antagonist" or when the "protagonist" lets them down.

Third person multiple is the best choice when you have a story in which you want to explore a big idea or develop an intricate plot. Often, you'll see authors of historical fiction, family sagas, social commentary novels, and big crime novels write in this POV. Think of Tom Wolfe (*The Bonfire of the Vanities*), E. L. Doctorow (*Ragtime*), and Dennis Lehane (*Mystic River*).

You can give information the protagonist doesn't have. You're not bound to present only what your main character experiences. This POV allows you to open up the world of the story and allows your readers to travel through the experiences of others.

Let's say your main character looks up to her boss and views her as the picture of success that she's striving to achieve. She sees her as "having it all": great husband, beautiful children, a fabulous house. With multiple POV, you get to show the reality: the stress the boss is under trying to maintain a facade of perfection, the kids who are out of control, the mountain of debt she's run up trying to maintain a lifestyle she can't afford, the husband who's never home. Being let in on both of these viewpoints allows the reader to get the whole picture. The boss now becomes more "human" with all the frailties that entails, and the employee seems naïve. The reader feels more sympathy for the boss and roots for the employee to gain wisdom—not just the corner office with the fat paycheck.

You can present conflicting viewpoints of the same events. This is an especially good advantage for mysteries. For instance, take the case of eye-witness accounts. You'd think because a person actually witnessed an event, that he or she would be able to say what happened with accuracy. Not true. The witness may have certain prejudices, bad eyesight, or be afraid to tell the truth. The people directly involved in the accident have their own perspectives on what happened. Invariably, it's always "the other guy's fault." Only by taking all these viewpoints into consideration do you get a full picture of what actually happened.

You can develop more complex characters. Because all the characters are not filtered through the lens of your main character—as with first person and limited third person—you are free to develop a number of characters from the inside out, by presenting the thoughts of those characters. Readers get to learn what makes them tick, their fears and desires. This makes for a richer experience for the reader.

You avoid the potential for tedium — not just on the part of the author, but on the reader. If a reader is not really interested in a particular character, at least she knows that the amount of time she'll be spending with that character is limited. It's like visiting your in-laws. You know eventually the visit will come to an end (for now), and then it's "so long, see you next time."

You can prolong suspense. Just as your readers think you're going one way, you do the unexpected and turn off the road. You can end a chapter on a cliffhanger. Instead of continuing the action in the next chapter, you can open with a different POV from another character in a different scene. This challenges readers' expectations, keeping them continually engaged to see where you'll take them next.

You can intensify dread. This was the feeling I had all the way through *The Memory Keeper's Daughter*. That's because there's a terrible secret at the heart of this novel. Two characters know the secret, but a third character doesn't. We keep waiting for that character to learn of the secret and wonder what her reaction will be. That sense of dread makes this a real page-turner.

But for all the many advantages of third person multiple, there are just as many drawbacks.

Drawbacks

You can lose the thread of the story. It's possible to get so caught up in hopping from one point of view to another that the basic plot gets lost.

The protagonist's journey can get muddled. When you've got more than one point of view, it means less "face time" for your protagonist. And that means less time to get into the personal issues she has to overcome by story's end. The hero's journey can become fragmented and muddled.

It's more difficult to include memories, flashbacks, and opinions. When you've got multiple characters all jockeying for story time, there's not a lot of time to include all those things that give a story dimension. You simply can't show or explain it all. Sometimes, the less said the better. Whatever you do decide to include, you've got to do it in such a way that it doesn't drag down the pacing.

There's the danger of readers not getting invested enough in any character. This can leave readers feeling unsatisfied, and they may lose interest in the story. That's why it's crucial to determine who your most important characters are and who your readers want to get to know better—and then to spend sufficient time with them.

The book can end up being too long. The more POV characters you have, the more "real estate" they will take up, and that can often result in a book that is too long to be marketable. A marketable length is usually between 75,000 words to 90,000 words for an adult novel.

WHEN CONSIDERING THIRD PERSON MULTIPLE, ASK YOURSELF:

Do each of my POV characters make a strong contribution to the story? Every POV character must have a compelling reason to tell their part of the story. They must each add a certain amount of complexity and understanding of events.

Will each of my POV characters have enough scenes? If you have POV characters appearing for one or two scenes and then disappearing, or being introduced very late in the story, it may be best to have those scenes in another character's POV. This is not necessarily a hard and fast rule, because there will be times when a crucial scene must be told from a character's POV only fleetingly. But you must have a compelling reason to do this and be able to handle it wisely.

Am I diluting the story of the main character by switching POVs? Remember: It's always about your main character. Even though there may be other POVs, the reader should be very clear whom this story is about.

Are each of my POV characters distinguished enough to be clear to the reader? For instance, if you've got two characters who are both Ivy League educated lawyers, they are not going to be *different* enough from each other to warrant their own POVs. It would be better to combine these characters into one.

Will I be able to create more suspense by using multiple POVs? This is absolutely key when you're writing a mystery or any novel with a secret at its core, such as *The Memory Keeper's Daughter*. Sometimes the suspense is rather thin, but by switching POVs you can prolong the suspense by withholding key information for a while.

Will the reader's experience be enhanced through multiple POVs? It's not good enough to choose third person multiple

POV just because you like the variety. It has to be because the story will be better told this way. Always remember your *readers*.

Examples of Bestsellers That Use Multiple POVs
The Memory Keeper's Daughter by Kim Edwards
Water for Elephants by Sarah Gruen
A Game of Thrones by George R. R. Martin

LESS COMMON POINTS OF VIEW

Certainly first person, third person limited, and third person multiple are not the only choices for POV. A number of other POV possibilities exist, though they are used much less often and can be very challenging for the writer to master. This is by no means a complete list, but the following points of view may give you some idea of the other options.

OMNISCIENT

This POV—sometimes referred to as the "God POV"—was very common in nineteenth-century literature. Today it's much less used. There's also more confusion that surrounds omniscient POV than any other POV.

Omniscient POV means that—like God—you as the author see all and know all. Therefore, you have the ability to enter into any and every character's thoughts and to experience the world through their senses. Moreover, you as the author can address the reader directly, offering up your comments and interpretations of what's happening between your characters. In essence, the author is "on stage," just as the Stage Manager is in Thornton Wilder's classic play, *Our Town*.

In *Tess of the d'Urbervilles*, for instance, Thomas Hardy describes his character like this: "Tess Durbeyfield at this time of her life was a mere vessel of emotion untinctured by experience." This is clearly the author's opinion, expressed to the reader.

Because of its unlimited flexibility, it would seem that the omniscient POV would be the easiest to master. Actually, it's the hardest. Because you are constantly reminding your reader that this is a work of fiction, you run the risk of alienating or even infuriating your readers. If not done skillfully, the author's intrusions can feel like the neighborhood busybody who has an opinion on everyone and everything. You just want her to shut up and disappear so you can go about your daily business.

Furthermore, with all the dipping in and out of character's heads, there's no one the reader can really invest in emotionally.

With all these reasons not to write in the omniscient, why on earth would an author choose this POV? Mainly, to offer insight into the characters and events taking place. The point of your novel, then, is not to create identification with any particular character, but to let the events of the novel speak for themselves so that your readers can come to their own conclusions.

Why you'd want to try it: Omniscient POV also allows the author to steer the reader toward the story's meaning more easily than other viewpoints. This viewpoint is ideal for satire or metafiction, the latter of which plays with the ideas of reality, fiction, and truth.

Warning: If you do choose to use the omniscient viewpoint, you must set it up very early in the story—ideally within the first few pages. And you need to be fully committed to this POV—you can't just drop in on a character's thoughts or insert your own interpretation of the action here and there. This POV will affect the entire style of your novel. Finally, because writing in this POV can startle readers who are used to more conventional viewpoints, you need to convince your readers early on that they will enjoy taking this journey with you. This requires you to have a strong style and command of your prose so your readers will trust you and go along for the ride.

Examples of Bestsellers That Use Omniscient POV
The Book Thief by Markus Zusak
The Lord of the Rings by J. R. R. Tolkien
Ender's Game by Orson Scott Card
The French Lieutenant's Woman by John Fowles

FIRST PERSON MULTIPLE

This POV is just like first person, except that you are offering the POV of several characters told from the POV of "I" (rather than "he" or "she").

Why you'd want to try it: You feel a strong need to get inside each of your character's heads—to show how an event has affected each one in a unique way. Rosellen Brown does this masterfully in her novel *Before and After*, about a family trying to hold itself together after a teenaged son murders his girlfriend.

Warning: Each character must have a distinct voice (vocabulary, syntax, rhythm of speech) and must be immediately identifiable. It's also a good idea to title the chapters with the characters' names so that readers don't get confused.

Examples of Bestsellers That Use First Person Multiple
Gone Girl by Gillian Flynn
Before and After by Rosellen Brown
My Sister's Keeper by Jodi Picoult

EPISTOLARY

This is actually a POV told entirely in the form of a journal or correspondence among characters. Alice Walker's novel *The Color Purple*, for instance, consists mostly of letters between Celie and her sister Nettie. Diary entries are another form of epistolary, as Carolly Erickson did in her novel, *The Hidden Diary of Marie Antoinette*, and Bram Stoker did in *Dracula*.

Other, more modern, ways to use epistolary include email, interoffice memos, and voice mail. (I do shutter to think, though, what a "texting" epistolary novel would read like!)

Why you'd want to try it: You want to fully explore emotion and the relationships between characters.

Warning: There's a danger of having nothing happen in your novel, of everything being recounted as a past event. The author's challenge is to bring immediacy and to find a way to recreate scenes as if they were playing in real time. (One way is for the writer of the letter or diary to write down her thoughts immediately following an event so that she can help sort out what happened in order to understand it.)

Examples of Bestsellers That Use Epistolary

The Hidden Diary of Marie Antoinette by Carolly Erickson
Bridget Jones's Diary by Helen Fielding
Dracula by Bram Stoker
The Perks of Being a Wallflower by Stephen Chbosky
Flowers for Algernon by Daniel Keyes

SECOND PERSON

This is the viewpoint of "you." In essence, the *reader* becomes the main character. Sometimes used in short stories, this POV is rarely used in novels. Jay McInerney did this to great effect in his bestselling novel, *Bright Lights, Big City.*

More often, authors may use this in a brief passage, as David Wroblewski does in *The Story of Edgar Sawtelle*, when Claude, the brother of Edgar's deceased father, spots the boy Edgar staring at him from a perch on a tree outside the kitchen window. Edgar has just discovered Claude's secret and wants to make sure Claude knows this. Rather than writing the scene from Claude's POV, the author creates a feeling of anxiety in the reader, which perfectly suits the moment in this story.

Why you'd want to try it: You want to force your readers to form a close identification with your protagonist. With second person, you involve the reader to the extreme, making the reader complicit in the action.

Warning: Readers might have exactly the opposite response you're looking for: *That's not me, I wouldn't think that way, act that way.*

Examples of Bestsellers That Use Second Person POV
Bright Lights, Big City by Jay McInerney
The Buddha in the Attic by Julie Otsuka

COMBO

Some authors—Michael Connelly and Lisa Gardner in particular—combine first person with third person.

Why you'd want to try it: This technique can be quite effective in mysteries and thrillers, when you want to get inside the criminal mind (or the victim's mind) and yet have the flexibility of third person.

Warning: This seems a lot easier than it is to pull off. You need to be very skillful so you don't irritate or confuse the reader.

Option: One way to do first person in Combo is by using the epistolary approach method to get inside another character's mind. For instance, Cody McFadyen intersperses the first person POV of Smoky Barrett in his novel *The Darker Side* with the diary of a victim, as well having sections written in the third person POV of another victim as told by the killer. In a lesser hand, this could be enormously confusing to the reader, but McFadyen uses his considerable skills in setting up each of the switches so they seem perfectly natural.

Examples of Bestsellers That Use Combo POVs
A Visit From the Goon Squad by Jennifer Egan
The Darker Side by Cody McFadyen
Touch & Go by Lisa Gardner

BEFORE MOVING ON

Play around with a few possibilities for POV. You can do this by writing a sample scene. Write it from first person POV, third person POV, or even some of the less common ones. See what feels right for you, and try to think ahead to your story's needs—and whether the POV you've chosen will support your story adequately.

AUTHOR INSIGHT

As discussed in this chapter, often an author's first impulse regarding POV is not necessarily the one that will serve the story best. One of the most frequent situations I come across is when a story that is told in the third person is simply not coming to life. In many cases, this is because the main character is so different from the author that the author cannot imagine writing as "I." In other cases, it's a way of distancing the author from a character with many flaws. And therein lies the problem. Writing in the third person is more distant than writing in the first person.

When one of my clients, Tom Farrell, first came to me, he had a completed draft of a thriller that was written in multiple POVs. While he had a good grasp of how to handle POV, I felt that the main character seemed awfully aloof. I just couldn't warm up to him. So, I suggested that Tom try writing the first chapter from the first person POV to see what happened. Here is what he said:

"When Diane suggested I try a rewrite in first person, I was somewhat reluctant. I was determined to continue with third person and 'get it right.' However, once I gave first person a shot, my main character came alive. I had the ability to portray inner conflict in a way that wasn't possible before. Certain incidents and plot twists flowed directly from character motivation in an easy and more convincing stream. The ability to unlock my main character on the page became a game changer."

—Tom Farrell, author of *The Kelso Club*

A POV PRIMER

First Person: The story is told from the POV of one character, using "I."

Third Person Limited: The story is told from the POV of one character, using "he" or "she."

Third Person Multiple: The story is told through several different characters.

Omniscient: Also known as the "God POV." The story is told through the voice of an unseen narrator who knows all and sees all.

Epistolary: The story is told in the form of a journal or correspondence among characters.

First Person Multiple: The story is told from the POV of multiple characters, but using the approach of first person ("I").

Second Person: The reader becomes the main character ("you").

Combo: The story is told both through first person POV and through third person POV.

6

WHO'S ALONG FOR THE RIDE?

Where Character Relationships Meet Story Arc

STORIES ARE ABOUT relationships: characters coming together and splitting apart, helping each other and hurting each other. As much as the journey of your main character is essential to build a solid story, it's the relationships your main character has to the other characters that will spark deep emotions, provoke conflict, and inspire change. When we think of the novels that stick with us long after we reach "the end," it's the relationships that we think of. Who would Scarlett O'Hara be without Rhett Butler? Anna Karenina without Count Vronsky? Clarice Starling without Hannibal Lecter? Jay Gatsby without Daisy Buchanan?

At this point, if you have been doing the process as I've laid out, you may feel that you have enough to sit down and start constructing the scenes for your novel. After all, you have a pretty good idea what your story is going to be about, who your main characters are and what they want, the Key Moments in your novel, and even what POV you'll be using. While this may be enough to start figuring out the remaining scenes in your novel, you need to give a little more thought to the relationships—what they are, how they will unfold, and how they will impact your main character's journey. This step will not only make that task of writing scenes easier, but will help to ensure that your novel has the depth necessary for a satisfying story. It will also help you to keep the tension high.

Coincidentally, this is often the step that most first-time novelists don't give much thought to. Pantsers might assume novels all contain organic relationships that develop naturally throughout the writing process. Plotters, on the other hand, assume that these relationships develop as a result of an author's carefully crafted plot. They bring in the relationships on an "as needed" basis to satisfy the needs of what they want to have happen in the novel.

The reality is, neither of these approaches will ensure dynamic character relationships. Preordaining character relationships is akin to having your mother set up a blind date for you because she thinks you two would make a perfect match. And while letting relationships develop organically is a good policy in real life, you'll get much better results in your novel if you do a little planning ahead of time on each and every relationship in your story.

> While letting relationships develop organically is a good policy in real life, you'll get much better results in your novel if you do a little planning ahead of time on each and every relationship in your story.

You read that right: it's not enough to know the arc of the main relationship (e.g., boy meets girl, boy gets girl, boy loses girl, yada yada yada …); you need to have a deep understanding of *all* the relationships and how they help or hinder your main character, as well as how the relationships evolve throughout the story.

There are two main types of relationships that help drive the story: the **Driving Relationship** and the **Opposing Relationship**. Additionally, there are two categories of relationships that help support the story: **friends, lovers** and **helpers** and **frenemies** and **foes**.

THE DRIVING RELATIONSHIP

Novels often involve many different relationships, and the main character can have relationships with dozens of other characters. But there is one relationship that stands out above all the others and helps to propel the story forward: **the Driving Relationship**. This is the relationship that is the most changeable, the most turbulent, the one that impacts your main character the most.

In a romance, this is most often the love relationship: Elizabeth Bennet and Mr. Darcy in *Pride and Prejudice*. In a serial killer thriller, it is most likely the investigator and the killer: any of the Alex Cross novels. In a legal thriller it would most probably be the client and the attorney: John Grisham's *The Client*. In *The Girl with the Dragon Tattoo*, the driving relationship is between the reporter

Mikael Blomkvist and the computer hacker Lisbeth Salander. In *To Kill a Mockingbird*, it's Scout and her father, Atticus.

Why is it so important to know the driving relationship?

Understanding this relationship will help you to make strong creative decisions as you develop your story. Here's what's important to know:

The driving relationship is the one relationship that embodies both the story concept and character. It is the clearest window into your main character's experience and is the one that helps propel the main character's journey.

If you're not sure which of your characters should be the character who drives the relationship, or the Driving Character, ask the following questions. Even if you are sure, answering these questions will help you to capitalize on this relationship to deepen your novel:

1. Which character forces the main character to confront her weaknesses or mistakes?

2. Which relationship changes in nature from the beginning of the story to the end?

3. Which character offers the best thematic window into the story?

4. Which relationship is the most interesting?

In *The Hunger Games*, there are multiple character relationships that might seem to be the driving relationship of the story. Several characters motivate the protagonist, Katniss Everdeen, to be a fierce competitor in the hunger games—but which one would we consider the Driving Relationship? Let's see how this would play out by answering each of the above questions.

1. Initially, it seems that Prim, Katniss's younger sister, forces Katniss to push through her weakness and self-doubt to bring food to her family, and to become a fierce contender in the competition. As the story progresses, however, it is Peeta who forces Katniss, more than any other character in the book, to persevere in the most difficult moments of the competition.

2. Unlike her relationship with her mother and Prim, Katniss's relationship with Peeta changes over the course of the story. In the beginning, Peeta is a virtually nonexistent figure in her life, connected to her only by the memory of sharing burnt bread. By the end of the games, they are linked romantically, politically, and, it seems, permanently to one another by their newfound celebrity.

3. The compassion with which Katniss and Peeta treat one another stands in stark contrast to the harsh world of Panem. Thematically, Collins uses this relationship to reveal the importance of caring for one another, and the ability to overcome extreme adversity by acting as fundamentally good and caring human beings. While Katniss's relationships with other characters are meaningful, the plot of the story requires that she spends the most time with Peeta, making their relationship an obvious choice for conveying these themes.

4. The driving force of *The Hunger Games*, for most readers, becomes the romantic relationship between Katniss and Peeta. In both the novel and film

adaptation, this budding relationship serves as the emotional core of the story, and ensures readers' long-term investment in the outcome of the competition.

THE DRIVING PROGRESSION

Once you've determined the Driving Relationship, it's time to figure out how that relationship is going to progress throughout the story. A typical Driving Progression has at least four stages: the Status Quo, the Shift, the Rupture, the Reunion. Let's take a look at each of them.

The Status Quo

This is not necessarily the introduction of characters, but the scene early on in which we see how these characters will act with each other under normal circumstances. The relationship might be flirtatious or antagonistic, that of mentor and mentee, "yes-man" to an overbearing boss, etc.

In *The Hunger Games*, we see the extreme distance between Peeta and Katniss, who hardly know each other. Peeta displayed compassion for her by secretly giving her bread when they were children, but their relationship doesn't develop beyond this moment. While it's clear that Katniss remembers his kindness as they get older, the relationship between the two characters is virtually nonexistent in the day-to-day life of District 12.

The Shift

Something happens between the characters that will change how they relate to each other (e.g., the first kiss, saving the other's life, standing up for the other, etc.). They can never go back to the way the relationship was before.

When Peeta is randomly selected as the other representative of their district, it is clear that the relationship between Peeta and Katniss is going to change. This shift occurs concretely in the moment that the duo is instructed to hold hands during their first public appearance as the tributes from District 12. They are marketed as both a team and a potential romantic partnership, and they begin to believe this vision themselves.

The Rupture

This is usually the lowest point for the main character—and is often the point at which the main character and the Driving Character have either had a falling out or get separated through an outside force (e.g., a lover walks out, a ward is kidnapped, a business partner disappears, etc.).

For Katniss, this rupture occurs when she discovers that Peeta has joined the Career tributes—highly trained competitors from the more affluent districts of Panem—in the competition. She feels a sense of betrayal and isolation, and she concludes that Peeta's affinity for her has been nothing but an act.

The Reunion

The characters come back together and resolve their relationship in one form or another.

The reunion of Katniss and Peeta occurs when Katniss, badly injured from lethal tracker jacker stings, tries to take the bow and arrow from a dead tribute. Peeta discovers her and warns her to run, just as Cato, the most volatile tribute, appears. Peeta distracts him, giving Katniss time to escape. In this moment, Katniss realizes that, in spite of his alliance with the Career tributes, Peeta truly has her safety in mind.

If you're writing a very complex novel, you may actually have more than one Driving Relationship. In that case, you will want to work out a progression for each. This will allow you to see clearly whether you actually need both relationships—or whether eliminating one (or severely cutting down on the character's role) can actually strengthen the role of the dynamic.

> If you're writing a very complex novel, you may actually have more than one Driving Relationship. In that case, you will want to work out a progression for each.

THE OPPOSING RELATIONSHIP

All good stories have an antagonist—or opponent—someone who is preventing your main character from reaching her goal, or is endangering her life or love, or is in some way making life very difficult for her. Paul Sheldon is terrorized by Annie Wilkes in *Misery*, Harry Potter is in constant opposition to Lord Voldemort, and even Jekyll has the alternate, evil personality of Hyde.

An opponent does not have to be malevolent. You can have a perfectly good, likeable opponent. The key is that this character is either pulling the main character away from his goals or pushing him toward something that will force him to grow.

> An opponent does not have to be malevolent. You can have a perfectly good, likeable opponent.

Presumably by now you have an opponent in mind and have done a Character Blueprint on him or her. But there's more work to be done!

To keep the stakes in your story high, to keep the plot humming along, you need to delve into the relationship of the main character to the opponent and how that *changes.* Like the Driving Relationship, the Opposing Relationship has a progression: the Status Quo, First Noose Tightening, Second Noose Tightening, the Battle. Let's explore this Opposing Progression:

The Status Quo

This is the first interaction of the main character with the opponent, where we will see what the main character is up against. Note: The main character may not know the opponent or may not even have any scene with the opponent until later in the story. If this is the case with your novel, the Status Quo is a good place to have the reader meet the opponent and learn what the main character is facing.

Let's take *The Silence of the Lambs* as an example. Before Clarice Starling is even introduced to Hannibal Lecter, she is warned that he is a highly manipulative, dangerous individual. Within minutes of their first meeting, Hannibal—who is in a high-security holding cell—manages to control Clarice's behavior, forcing her to step very close to his cell and reveal her badge and credentials. Hannibal's ability to manipulate her establishes an unexpected status quo, in which he is able to control both his surroundings and Clarice—even when his physical agency is limited. Along with Clarice, the reader learns just what she's up against.

First Noose Tightening

The opponent's activity is ramped up, making life *very difficult* for your main character.

In *The Silence of the Lambs*, the first noose tightening comes during their initial meeting, when Hannibal refuses to fill out

Clarice's questionnaire. Realizing that Clarice needs his help to profile Buffalo Bill, Hannibal tightens the noose of their relationship by only giving her information on his terms. He sends her away with cryptic clues, which she has no choice but to attempt to decipher.

Second Noose Tightening

The opponent's activity is heightened even more, making life *nearly impossible* for your main character.

The second definitive noose tightening comes when Clarice visits Hannibal again, desperate for information, and Hannibal refuses to help her unless she can get him moved to a different location, where he might be able to be outdoors. Again, Hannibal puts a roadblock in Clarice's efforts to find Buffalo Bill, and she is forced to comply with his wishes.

Note: You may have more than two nooses. Thrillers and adventure stories, especially, have many more than two. A more literary novel might have only two—but that's the *least* you should have in your story. The point is that the opponent needs to ratchet up the stakes, making life harder and harder for your main character.

The Silence of the Lambs has countless noose tightening moments, each time Hannibal exerts mental control over Clarice by making demands before he'll give her further information. Perhaps the most famous noose tightening occurs when Hannibal forces Clarice to share the story of her childhood attempt to save a lamb from being slaughtered. After Clarice shares this story with Hannibal, he simply tells her that all the information she needs is in her case files. Clarice is then driven to study the files intensely, hoping to rescue Catherine Martin before it's too late. Throughout the story, Hannibal, as the opponent, influences and impedes the main character's actions.

The Battle

This is the moment your main character confronts the opponent—either directly or indirectly—and fights to the finish. This is where your main character calls on his strength or skills to vanquish his opponent, thereby also overcoming his central problem. The Battle Scene doesn't necessarily have to be a physical battle—or even a major blowout. It can be quiet. The key is that this scene needs to have tension and deep emotional impact. It is really the turning point in your story.

> The Battle Scene doesn't necessarily have to be a physical battle—or even a major blowout. It can be quiet. The key is that this scene needs to have tension and deep emotional impact. It is really the turning point in your story.

You might assume that the battle scene between Clarice and Hannibal occurs just after she divulges the story of the lamb, when she yells for him to give her Buffalo Bill's real name. It is, after all, a tense moment of face-to-face interaction between the main character and her opponent. In actuality, though, in the moment that Clarice identifies Buffalo Bill, she is truly defeating Hannibal and the control he has exerted over her for the duration of the novel. As she discovers the killer's identity and puts a stop to his murderous existence, Clarice no longer needs Hannibal to feed her information—and, consequently, Hannibal loses most of his control over Clarice. Of course, as Hannibal escapes and roams free in the world, there is the looming threat that he may seek her out eventually—a cliff hanger which is, in itself, a final noose tightening to keep the suspense of the story going well beyond the last page of the novel.

OTHER RELATIONSHIPS

ANSWER THE FOLLOWING QUESTIONS FOR *EVERY* CHARACTER:

- What is the essence of the relationship between this character and the main character?
- What purpose does this character serve?
- How does this relationship contribute to or reflect on the theme of the story?

Other than the most minor "walk on" characters, every single character in your novel needs to have a clear purpose. That means that they need to be more than just "sounding boards" for your main character. They need to agitate, provide contrast, create friction, teach, cause emotional turmoil, cause your character to question her thinking or actions or values, incite action, etc.

Generally, I like to divide the secondary characters into two groups:

1. **Friends, lovers, and helpers.** These are the characters who are sympathetic to your main character and who will help her in her journey. Essentially, these are the "good guys."

Examples:

Ron Weasley and Hermione Granger in the Harry Potter series
Samwise Gamgee in *The Lord of the Rings*
Dr. Watson in the Sherlock Holmes series

2. **Frenemies and foes.** These are all the characters who are getting in the way of your main character, making life difficult, backstabbing, pretending to

be on the side of your main character but really out for themselves, working for the opponent, etc.

Examples:

Peter Pettigrew in the Harry Potter series

Fernand Mondego in *The Count of Monte Cristo*

Claudius and Gertrude in *Hamlet*

Put each of your secondary characters into one or the other category. (If you find your lists being very lopsided, this is a good indication that you may need to add or subtract some characters on each side.)

BEFORE MOVING ON

Once you've deepened the relationships with your characters, go back to your Story Blueprint and see whether any of these moments fit in with the Key Moments. You may find that this is just what you needed to deepen and strengthen some Key Moments that may have been lacking.

In other cases, you'll find that the character progressions will fit either just before or just after a Key Moment.

In the next chapter we're going to be putting all this work to good use—creating a Scene Stack of every scene in your novel.

THE DRIVING RELATIONSHIP

The Status Quo: How the characters relate to each other under normal circumstances.

The Shift: Something happens between the characters that changes their relationship.

The Rupture: The characters have a falling out or are otherwise kept apart.

The Reunion: The characters reunite and resolve their relationship.

THE OPPOSING RELATIONSHIP

The Status Quo: We learn what the main character is up against.

First Noose Tightening: The opponent ramps up his activity.

Second Noose Tightening: The opponent makes life even more difficult for the main character.

The Battle: The main character confronts the opponent.

7

THE SCENE STACK
Building Your Story Scene by Scene

ALL NOVELS ARE made up of scenes. Like a mason laying down bricks, the fiction writer uses scenes to build her novel—scene by scene, brick by brick. The scenes, like floors of a building, become chapters: either one scene per chapter, several scenes per chapter, or one scene that stretches out over multiple chapters. At this point, you only need concern yourself with the scenes.

Each scene moves the story along in a significant way. A scene can be quiet and reflective or filled with action. It can contain just one character—or an entire battlefield. But the key point to keep in mind is that every scene in your novel must have a clear *raison d'être*, or reason for being in there.

> Every scene in your novel must have a clear *raison d'être*, or reason for being in there.

Too often, I've seen writers hammer out scenes that, while engaging, did not clearly advance the story. When I bring this up to them—"This scene doesn't really belong here. It's good, but the story is stalling"—I usually get some variation of this response: "But I like that scene. And it took me a month to write it." I see this happen most often with pantsers. They will get inspired to write a scene because of something that inspires them, without any regard to how the scene fits into the whole of the piece. Plotters, on the other hand, have usually thought out their scenes very carefully, leaving no room for serendipity.

I'm sure you're itching to start writing your scenes. But before you dive in, you need to be clear *why* you have each scene and *what* precisely will happen. Basically you need to answer the six journalist questions: who, what, when, where, why, and how? But there's one more "W" question that's absolutely crucial to answer in every scene: *want*. What does your character want and what's standing in her way? This is the question that provides the tension in the scene. The three-step process in this chapter will help you get there.

STEP 1: GENERATE A LIST OF SCENES

By now you know enough about your characters and your story to come up with a list of possible scenes. Notice I said "possible." Don't censure yourself at this point. Write down any and every idea that comes to mind—no matter how ridiculous it may seem at the moment. Aim to come up with anywhere between fifty to one hundred scenes. This is just going to be a very basic list from which you will eventually create your Scene Stack.

Distill into one to three lines what happens in the scene. Be sure to include your Key Moments and circle them.

You're going to distill into one to three lines what happens in the scene. When doing this, be sure to include your Key Moments and circle them. For now, don't worry about the order of the scenes or whether they will ultimately make it into your novel. This step is simply to generate ideas. Here's what a list might look like:

1. John asks Mary out on a date. Mary turns him down.

2. John sees Mary at the farmer's market and asks her advice about a new food product.

3. Mary rushes her chronically ill child to the ER.

4. John argues with a female co-worker.

Notice how basic—and, yes, bland—each scene seems. Right now, we're just looking at the essence, the big *what* of each scene. Keep in mind that at this point you may have more scenes than will actually make it into your novel. That's more than okay. This is not the time to discard any ideas or scenes—no matter how far-fetched they may at first seem to you.

This is not the time to discard any ideas or scenes—no matter how far-fetched they may at first seem to you.

So, where do you get your list of scenes? Look at the Key Moments, the Driving Progression, and the Opposing Progression. That's a great start. Each of these moments should be filled with drama, conflict, and change, moving your story forward. Don't be surprised if you have some overlap. For instance, the Happening in your story may actually coincide with the Shift of the Driving Progression.

Next, look at all the questions you asked and presumably answered of your main character and supporting characters. That should help you generate ideas for scenes, even if you're not sure just yet where they go. The idea is to not censure yourself at this point. You want to open your mind to all the possibilities. Don't be afraid to think big and off the wall. If you suddenly think, *Wouldn't it be great if there was a scene where Jason got attacked by a wolf,* and your story happens to be set in New York City, go with it! There's a reason your mind came up with that seemingly crazy idea. Later on, you can always discard it.

STEP 2: MAKE A SCENE STACK

Now that you have your list of scenes, it's time to flesh them out a bit more and begin to answer those five journalist questions. You're going to literally create a stack of scenes on index cards, with one card per scene. If you've got more than one POV character in your novel, you'll want to get a stack of colored index cards—one color per character. This will help you keep track of whose POV you're in at any given moment.

Each card will contain the following information: Who is in the scene, when it takes place, where it takes place, what happens, why the scene is in the novel, how it will be approached, what your POV character wants, and what's standing in his or her way. That's everything you will need for a scene to work. Let's explore each one of these elements in detail:

WHO is in the scene.

This is your *dramatis personae*. Include all important characters. If you are writing in multiple POVs, then write the POV character's name for that scene at the top.

You don't need to include minor characters, unless you need to plant them in the scene for later use. For instance, if you are writing a murder mystery and a major suspect appears only fleetingly in an early scene, you'll probably want to include that as an establishing fact. This will help you to keep track of where your important characters are at all times.

WHEN it takes place.

You can include a general sense of the time (e.g., early evening in late summer) or a very specific time (e.g., 3:00 on Friday, the day after the murder). What you put will depend on the particular constraints of your story. It will also help you to see if your timeline makes sense, once you begin to lay out the scenes.

Note: You can have a scene take place in more than one setting as long as the action is continuous (e.g., the characters are walking out of their office, riding the elevator, exiting the building into the parking lot, and driving home). But if you skip from one place (the office) to the next (the car), that constitutes two separate scenes.

WHERE the scene takes place.

Besides helping you to keep track of logistics, you'll be able to see whether you need to create more—or fewer—settings.

WHAT happens in the scene.

This is going to be a very simple description—only a few lines at most. You are looking for the essence of what this scene is about. Focus on the central conflict of the scene. For instance,

"Kylie tries to convince her mother that she should be allowed to travel to Europe alone. Her mother absolutely refuses, and Kylie storms out of the house."

WHY this scene is in the novel.

You must show a clear purpose for every single scene in your story, whether it's to reveal an important clue, to show a side of a character that others don't see, to set up a dangerous situation for a character, to show the aftermath of a horrible fight, etc.

HOW the scene will be approached.

Will it be quiet, emotionally charged, nail biting, hilarious? Knowing how the scene will be handled can help you to see — once you've put the scenes in order — whether you've got too many action-packed scenes on top of each other, or not enough action.

What does your character WANT and what's standing in her way?

Want is what drives a scene and what creates conflict and tension. Without want, there really is no scene. For instance, let's look at the possible scene mentioned earlier in this chapter: John sees Mary at the farmer's market and asks her advice about a new food product. Since Mary had already turned him down for a date in the previous scene, his "want" in this scene may be to get Mary to see him in a positive light. Maybe she had turned him down because she thought he was too much of a know-it-all. By asking her advice, he is showing her that he's open to others' opinions.

But what could be standing in his way? Perhaps another shopper (maybe an older woman) chimes in and offers her opinion, and he shoots her down. Or maybe Mary acts suspicious of his motives.

Both options show a clear *want* (to be seen in a better light) and an *obstacle*.

To show you how this process plays out, I've taken a scene from Kim Edwards's *The Memory Keeper's Daughter*. In this novel, the character of Norah has just given birth to twins in her husband's medical office. What she doesn't know is that one of the babies was born with Down Syndrome. While she is asleep, her husband, David, makes a life-changing decision to give the baby to his nurse to take to an institution.

NORAH

WHO: Norah; her newborn, Paul; her husband, David.

WHEN: Winter of 1964, following a snowstorm; nearly dusk the day after she's given birth.

WHERE: The building entrance of the medical office where David works.

WHAT: Norah (carrying Paul) and David leave the medical office where she had given birth the night before. Norah asks to see the infant girl who she believes died at birth. David tells her she can't, that she's been taken away to be buried.

WHY: To establish the lie.

HOW: Quiet, gentle, full of unspoken emotion.

CHARACTER WANT: To have closure on her baby's death.

OBSTACLE: David's evasiveness.

STEP 3: CREATE A SCENE PROGRESSION

Now that you've got your Scene Stack, it's time to position the cards in the order you think they might go. At this point, don't worry yet about how they will work as chapters. We're just looking to see how the scenes themselves unfold to tell the story.

Clear a space either on a table or the floor, then lay out the cards side by side. Be sure to signify the Key Moment so it stands out visually. Using the example of *The Memory Keeper's Daughter*, with a Key Moment of the Happening in the second scene and with Caroline as the POV character, here is how it should look:

Now, without judgment, read each card in the order you've laid them out. Then ask yourself the following questions:

Is there enough variety of settings to keep the reader interested?

If not, can you change any of the settings to be more interesting? The setting should enhance the scene, not keep it constrained. If you have too many indoor scenes, ask how you can bring some of them outdoors. Make bold choices: instead of having two characters meet in their office to discuss an important take-down of a rival, how about setting it at a local deli or as the characters stroll through a museum?

Does the scene have a clear purpose?

It's not enough for a scene to be emotional or funny or colorful or scary. It must have a reason to be in your novel. In my work with authors, too often I have read scenes that seemed more like window dressing than integral parts of the story. In these cases, the scene might be interesting in and of itself, but it leaves the reader scratching her head, wondering why the author put it there.

Note: Before you write any scene, ask yourself how it serves your story. Each scene either should help a particular character move closer to his ultimate goal or should put up obstacles, creating a struggle. If the scene does not have a clear purpose, ask, "Can I eliminate the scene or change it?"

Are there scenes that essentially duplicate each other?

You want to make sure that every scene offers the reader something new. If you have two battle scenes, for instance, they must have a very different purpose. One of my authors had written a terrific dystopian novel in which a number of battle scenes occurred. While the scenes were meticulously rendered, it was difficult to tell one battle from the other. So, together we worked on combining some battles, completely eliminating others, and finding a different goal for each battle to accomplish in terms of the main character's journey. Now, each battle is clearly defined and, hopefully, memorable to the reader.

If you find yourself in a similar situation, ask if you can eliminate one or more of the scenes, combine them, or find something new to highlight.

Is there enough "space" between the Key Moments?

You want to avoid a lopsided structure. Make sure that your Key Moments are not crammed up against each other and that you don't have too many long stretches between the Key Moments. This is important to keep the pacing of your story flowing.

Is the order of scenes the most effective?

Here's where you can try risk-free reordering to see if the story is more effective with the scenes arranged differently. Don't be afraid to mix up the time frame. Just be sure your readers won't get lost.

One of my clients had a story that was set in three different time periods. However, the story could not be told chronologically. The challenge for him was in finding a way to order the scenes so that each scene revealed something that moved the journey for the main character forward—even though the timeline was all mixed up. By laying the scenes out next to each other, we could see clearly the thematic elements and where the conflicts would be most effective.

Does the timeline make sense?

Pay attention to the WHEN and the WHERE on your cards. Ask yourself if you're cramming too many events into too short a time frame or if you have long stretches of unaccounted-for time?

In looking specifically at the timeline with one of my clients after she had laid out all the scene cards, it suddenly became clear that she had created the equivalent of a 72-hour day! There was simply no believable way that her character could get from one location to another, and then to another and another in one day.

Do I have too many POV characters?

Aim for no more than five. If you have more, ask yourself who can be eliminated or combined into another character. Stick to one POV per scene. When choosing which character to use, ask, "Who has the most to lose or gain?" Once you answer that, it should become obvious whose POV to choose.

If I'm writing in multiple POVs, is there a good balance?

Do some POV characters get lost for too many scenes? Is the order of scenes too repetitive (Character A, Character B, Character

C, Character A, Character B, Character C, etc.)? Do you have too many scenes in one character's POV and not enough in another character's POV?

Do each of the scenes feel as though they are moving the story forward?

You should have a sense of one thing leading to another and of mounting conflict and tension.

READ ALOUD YOUR SCENE PROGRESSION

Once you feel fairly satisfied with your scene progression, tell the story of your novel by reading aloud the cards and recording it. This is an absolutely revelatory step.

I remember the first time I had an author do this while we were working together. John had come to me with only a bare-bones synopsis, some character histories, and a couple of chapters. After two intensive days of working together, we laid down a scene progression for the entire novel. The cards reached from one end of the room to the other. We were lucky enough to have a wall-to-wall desk/shelf in the room.

We were both exhausted from the work and felt really good about how the story had shaped up. But I wanted to be sure. And—I wanted John to be sure. So, I asked him to read back the cards. What happened was truly amazing! John wasn't just slavishly reading what he had written on the card; he was actually telling me the story of his novel. It was flowing beautifully.

But sure enough, there were a few places where the scenes felt stalled, or duplicated, or in the wrong order. And there were one or two places that we felt needed an additional scene. Even more important, John was able to make connections between events at various places in his novel so that he could deepen the themes and the depth of his story. This step also resulted in finding an ending for the novel that felt perfect.

Reading aloud your scene progression—and recording it if you can—will give you a sense of satisfaction. You may not have written any actual scenes yet, but you do have the story in place.

BEFORE MOVING ON

Very important: Before you stack up your scene cards, be sure to clearly number them!

AUTHOR INSIGHT

Here's what I got from the Scene Stack process:

Organization. It's the first time since I have started this book that I have felt that I am putting together a framework that will lead to The End.

Liberation. The Scene Stack doesn't mean that I would squash any creativity about going where the muse leads. Instead, it offers me a structure on which to let my imagination soar. It also points out where there are some weaknesses. The process helped me realize that some of what I had already written was too easy for the characters, and all was sweetness and light. The cards helped me focus on the conflict, showed room to grow, and greatly helped with the pacing.

Now that I know about this novel-writing process, I feel like I will finally stop wandering in the wilderness, writing one scene after another, with no end in sight.

—Katherine Rapp, writing student

SCENE TEST

Ask yourself the following questions for each and every scene:

- Is there enough variety of settings to keep the reader interested?
- Does the scene have a clear purpose?
- Are there scenes that essentially duplicate each other?
- Is there enough "space" between the Key Moments?
- Is the order of scenes the most effective?
- Do I have too many POV characters?
- If I'm writing in multiple POVs, is there a good balance?
- Do each of the scenes feel as though they are moving the story forward?

8

WRITING FAST AND UGLY

The Beauty of the Sketch Draft

THINK OF A novel as a complex painting. Writers construct scenes like artists sketch portraits. When confronted with a blank page, the artist first establishes the framework of the image by briefly sketching where each element of the face should be placed. He draws the general head shape, the shoulders, and the structural relationship of the eyes, ears, nose, and mouth before getting too detailed. If he decides to focus on the eyelashes or pupils first, the whole portrait will likely be unbalanced by the time he gets all the other elements of his subject's face onto the paper.

A Sketch Draft is no different—it's a portrait of your scene. It sketches the most critical components of your story, and ensures that they all combine into what will eventually be a much more thoroughly detailed piece of writing.

This step is a final way for you to lay out the bare bones of your plot before you get caught up in the flashy stuff: flowery descriptions, dialogue, etc. We'll get into exactly how to fill out your writing with more literary flourishes later on.

The Sketch Draft is your story in miniature—makes sense, right? It is essentially a stripped-down version of your novel. It contains everything that happens—but without the art and style.

> ## The Sketch Draft is your story in miniature. It is essentially a stripped-down version of your novel. It contains everything that happens—but without the art and style.

Put another way, think of the Sketch Draft as an outfit without all the accessories. Let's face it: it's the accessories that make (or break) an outfit. But you can't go out into public wearing only scarves and shoes! But this is the very problem that writers get into. They rush into writing their novels, dressing them up with all sorts of beautiful language, nifty dialogue, and funny and sad moments—without making sure that what they're hanging all this "writing" on is sound.

I've seen this happen over and over with the authors who come to me looking for help. They've been told that their writing is beautiful, wonderful, evocative, funny, or whatever, but that the story is just not coming together. They know something's off, but they don't know what it is. When I dive in and start to see what's going on, often I find that the scenes have not been constructed carefully.

As a writer, you'll have one of either two reactions to being asked to create a Sketch Draft. The pantsers among you will feel frustration that you can't really write the scene, while plotters will be relieved that you can get the scene on paper without having to worry about really "writing" it. Both responses are normal and perfectly fine. However, if your response is one of frustration, please bear with this step and you'll find that conquering your Sketch Draft will help you get to a final draft with much less angst—and in much shorter time.

Tackling your Sketch Draft at this point in writing your novel accomplishes two things:

1. It eliminates getting stuck down the road.

2. It helps you see very clearly what's working and what's not working in your novel.

BEAT BY BEAT

The Sketch Draft is essentially a beat-by-beat breakdown of your novel. Novels are made up of scenes, and scenes are made up of beats. Beats are those big moments in which something changes: the moment a character falls in love or knows the relationship has ended, decides to make a change in her life, or takes a huge risk. Then, there are the smaller beats or moments: a character catches another in a lie, realizes she's made a mistake, confronts another character, helps another character. Think of beats as mini turning points, or moments that invite more action to unfold and move the plot forward.

> Think of beats as mini turning points, or moments that invite more action to unfold and move the plot forward.

All scenes have an architecture, which in a way echoes the architecture of the novel as a whole: the Happening, the Choice, Moment of Truth, Final Confrontation, and New Reality. (Of course, some of your scenes may be broken into pieces and meted out for drama's sake.)

Your Sketch Draft should highlight each of these elements of your scene—like each foundational feature the artist draws in his initial portrait.

UNDERSTANDING YOUR SKETCH DRAFT

You're going to be using your Scene Stack to create your Sketch Draft. What you're looking to write are the major beats of each scene. But before you fire up your computer, consider these points:

What You Won't Be Writing

- Descriptions (except where *absolutely* necessary)

- Internal thoughts of characters (unless it involves a shift that changes things)

- Every bit of dialogue

- Dialogue tags (he said, she asked, etc.)

- Detailed action

- Transitions

- Observations, musings

- Metaphors, similes, beautifully crafted sentences

Okay, I know what you're thinking: So, what *is* left to write?

What You <u>Do</u> Write

- The moments, the beats, the important pieces of dialogue and action that move us through the scene

- The beginning, middle, and end—the nuts and bolts

HOW TO CREATE A SKETCH DRAFT

Remember that Scene Stack you created? That's going to be the basis for your Sketch Draft. Here's what you do:

Step One: Group the scenes into chapters.

Spread your Scene Stack out before you in the order in which you numbered your scenes. Study the scenes to determine how they may be grouped into chapters.

There's really no hard and fast rule here; some authors write a lot of very short chapters, others write fewer, longer chapters. If you have some very short scenes interspersed with other longer scenes, it might be a good idea to group those into one chapter.

Some chapters may contain more than one scene; and some scenes may play out over the course of two or more chapters. There's no right or wrong way to determine what constitutes a chapter, though there should be a sense of change from the beginning to the ending and a feeling that something is uniting the scenes. Frankly, this is one place where you can really trust your instincts.

However, you do want to make sure each chapter ends in a way that makes the reader want to read on to the next chapter.

Step Two: Make a note of the larger beats of each scene.

You'll find these in your brief description of the WHAT. For instance, let's go back to our example of John and Mary from the previous chapter. Looking at the scene—John sees Mary at the farmer's market and asks her advice about a new food product—you can immediately see two big beats:

1. John sees Mary.
2. John asks Mary's advice.

But there are many more smaller beats in that scene. For instance:

1. John arrives at the farmer's market.
2. While purchasing ears of corn, John spots Mary over at a condiment booth.
3. John quickly pays for his purchase and wends his way through the crowd of shoppers to Mary.
4. John picks up a jar of some exotic salsa and pretends to be interested in it.
5. John asks Mary if she's ever tried the salsa.
6. Mary smiles and says, "No."
7. John picks up another jar and says, "How about this?"
8. And so on, and so forth until you get to the end of the scene, which may be Mary looking for a quick escape from John!

Step Three: Sketch in your draft.

Using the beats you determined in Step Two, begin to write your draft. Write as quickly as you can, just hitting those beats. Avoid trying to make it look pretty. Your Sketch Draft is going to be for your eyes only.

Let's take a look at how this might play out. First, here's a fully rendered passage from one of my clients, Joanne Tombrakos's novel, *The Secrets They Kept*:

[Kristina] heard the phone ring, but made no move to answer it. She was certain it was Elena. That was her daughter, always wanting to know everything. But she couldn't talk about this. She wouldn't know where to begin. The answering machine would pick up, the one she never wanted that Elena bought for her so she would stop staying home waiting for phone calls. Now she used it to screen who she wanted to talk to.

Here's how this passage might look in a Sketch Draft:

Kristina heard the phone ring. She was certain it was Elena. But she couldn't talk about this. So, she let the answering machine pick up.

Notice how all the background about her relationship with her daughter and how she used the answering machine is not in here. All we have is the beat: the phone rings with a call from her daughter; Kristina decides to let the answering machine pick up. That's it. That's all we need to know—*for now*. That's the beat, clear and simple, without the exposition, relationship, and beautiful language to get in the way.

A SAMPLE SKETCH DRAFT SCENE

Building a Sketch Draft from your scene cards is only difficult if you allow yourself to be caught up with small details. As you sit down to write, don't give yourself too much time. You'll likely have lots of images, lines of dialogue, and specific word choices you desperately want to include as you begin to envision your scene, but that's not what the Sketch Draft is about. You need to make sure your scene is structurally sound, hitting the beats of your story. Let's see how this process might play out in an entire scene.

Throughout this and the next couple of chapters, we're going to be following one scene from a work-in-process by Brianna Flaherty. Here's a sample scene pulled from a Scene Stack. For our purposes, we will name the scene "The Best Intensions." Eleanor Slade is an elderly woman and John is her mid-forties son.

SCENE CARD: THE BEST INTENSIONS
POV: JOHN

Who: John and his mother, Eleanor.

When: November 2005, just after Halloween.

Where: Local diner in a rural Georgia town.

What: John meets his mother at a diner to give her an ultimatum. They talk about why she hasn't seen her grandchildren. He asks her to move into a nursing home.

Why: To establish Eleanor's mental instability, and the distance that's grown between John and his mother and her grandchildren.

How: A tense conversation, masked by small talk.

Want: To have a better relationship with his mother and to build a relationship between her and her grandchildren.

Obstacle: John's fear of hurting her; Eleanor's denial.

Sketch Draft for "The Best Intensions"

Eleanor slid into the diner booth. John was watching the kids in the diner react to her appearance.

E: "Where are the grandbabies?"

J: "Soccer practice."

John felt guilty for lying.

E: "Why didn't they come by on Halloween?"

J: "We were in a different neighborhood."

John continued making small talk.

E: "Tell me why they didn't come."

J: "I couldn't get them past the gate."

John contemplated whether his mother knew the real reason—that all the kids in the neighborhood thought her house was haunted and all their parents thought she was a crazy old woman. He recalled trying to convince friends to come over to his house when he was a child.

J: "The kids really missed you, though."

Children were staring at Eleanor from across the diner, ducking behind the booth as she made eye contact. They were whispering the word "witch." John wasn't sure if his mother could hear them.

E: "They hate me, don't they?"

J: "They're afraid of you—of the house. I wish they weren't. The other kids told them it's haunted."

E: "Don't be ridiculous."

John was surprised she denied it, and he pointed out that the children in the diner were hiding from her. Eleanor started to cry.

John immediately wished he hadn't said anything. He watched her crumple her napkin in her hand. The children ran fast past their booth on their way out, and parents kept their eyes down.

J: "The kids have a game on Friday, if you want to come by."

She didn't respond.

One of the kids smacked his hand against the window by their booth and ran away into the parking lot screaming.

While this draft may look flat and a little clunky, Brianna did exactly what the Sketch Draft called for. We can see the natural progression of beats in the scene (*Eleanor slides into the booth and asks about her grandchildren; John lies about where they are*, etc.). We also see the conflict and tension, and we get an overall shape of the scene.

Remember: The Sketch Draft is not a reflection of you as a writer. It's for you, and you alone. This is merely to get you to put in the framework of your chapters so you have a sound structure upon which to create beautiful scenes. Write fast, write ugly, and trust that, moving forward, your story will clearly unfold.

> The Sketch Draft is not a reflection of you as a writer. It is merely to get you to put in the framework of your chapters so you have a sound structure upon which to create beautiful scenes.

TEST YOUR SKETCH DRAFT

Once you've gotten about halfway through writing your Sketch Draft, test it out. If you're really struggling, it's possible that you may be getting bogged down in "writing" your chapters, rather than "structuring" them. Also, this is when it's crucial to make sure that you're not summarizing your chapters, but really isolating those beats, or mini turning points. Let's take a look at the various things you might be doing to slow your progress. See if any of the following sounds true for you:

Do you find yourself getting hung up on finding the right words?

Remember: We're not looking for perfect language here, only the bare bones of each chapter. Just get it out on the page. If you get stuck trying to decide if your character drives to the market, takes a cab or walks, just say, "goes." Don't waste time on the details.

Are you writing backstory in any of your chapters?

There's a place for backstory—just not in the Sketch Draft. Keep to what happens in the present of each scene.

Does your dialogue go on too long?

We only need enough dialogue to move us from one beat to the next; we don't need nuance. Think in terms of the beginning and end of a conversation.

Are you getting hung up on internal thoughts of characters?

Write only those thoughts that move the plot forward.

Is your action very detailed?

In the Sketch Draft, we need just enough to know what happens—not every step it takes to get there. Instead of, "Tom stalked the side of the building and reached down to tie his shoe before frantically realizing he was in the sniper's path," just say, "Tom almost gets shot; realizes he's a dead man."

Do any of your characters spend time musing or making observations?

Include these only if they actually move the plot forward. For instance, it's only essential to know what Maggie added to her shopping list if one of those items triggers something that causes her to make a big decision.

Does each chapter have a clear beginning, middle, and end?

Really, that's the most important part. Check this two, three, four times!

Are you rereading any of your Sketch Draft chapters and thinking, *This sucks*?

Of course it sucks; it's a Sketch Draft, not a real chapter. Going back to our artist example, no artist in the sketch stage of creating a painting would think, *This picture is ugly*. No, the artist would instead say, "That tree in the background is too close to the subject," or, "That corner feels a little empty," or, "I have a great idea to bring out the sadness in the little girl's eyes." See what I mean? The artist knows it's a process of layering to get to a beautiful painting. Likewise, the novelist knows that beautiful stories don't just happen—they have to be carefully constructed. That's what we're aiming to do with this Sketch Draft. Besides, now is not the time to be rereading. We just want to keep pushing forward to get to the end.

AUTHOR INSIGHT

I'd made it my entire writing career believing I was a plotter. I plan things out, and writing a scene can take me hours. Well, it turns out, I have a lot more of the "pantser" in me than I previously thought—or so I learned through the Sketch Draft process.

The instructions were so simple: I just needed a framework for my scene. And yet I spent more time than I'm willing to admit staring blankly at my computer screen, unable to conjure the critical details and lines of dialogue I needed to get into my Sketch Draft. I found myself vividly imagining the entire scene and writing it out in my head, but I couldn't pinpoint the individual beats—or mini turning points—of my story.

Eventually, I figured out how to filter my imagination so that I could pull out the beats of the scene; the first images and lines that came into my mind wound up being the critical beats.

The process really helped me iron out the scene and determine its true function in my larger story. Had I not done the Sketch Draft, I have a feeling this scene would be undergoing far more revision than it will need now.

Moving forward, I think I'll be able to conjure a Sketch Draft with much more ease than I could before, which ultimately means that my scene will get constructed faster and more solidly than if I'd just written the whole thing on the fly. All in all, there were some definite growing pains; but it paid off, and I think it will continue to benefit my writing in the future.

—Brianna Flaherty

BEFORE MOVING ON

Take a two-week break. Put aside reading and writing in favor of more physical activity. This will allow your brain to rest so you make new connections.

SKETCH DRAFT REMINDERS

While constructing your Sketch Draft, avoid getting hung up on the following:

- Trying to find the right words
- Writing backstory
- Nuanced dialogue
- Internal thoughts of characters
- Detailed action
- Musings, observations
- Self-judgments about your writing

9

THE WTF* DRAFT
Putting Emotion into Your Story
*Write the Feelings

CONGRATULATIONS! YOU'VE GOTTEN through the toughest part of the novel-writing process: the Sketch Draft. No doubt you're probably finding your Sketch Draft lacking. That's more than okay. In fact, the purpose of this draft is to put up a clear framework for each scene so that you can judge its effectiveness without being distracted by "beautiful" writing.

I've had more than one of my clients call in despair after reading their Sketch Draft, saying one version or another of this refrain: "I suck as a writer." But in the same way a pencil sketch that precedes a painting is not a finished work of art, the Sketch Draft is not an accurate reflection of your writing. It's about structure, story, and getting the whole framework in place before getting to the "good" stuff.

Think of it another way: if you've ever seen a house built or gone through the agony of renovation—as I have too many times to count—things look pretty ghastly until the decorating stage. It's nothing you'd ever want to show off to company, unless they happen to be contractors. But it's all necessary work. Yet, face it: for most people it's the decorating that's the fun part; that's where you get to put your personal stamp on a room, make it reflect who you are as a person.

Put all the emotion, all the stuff you really want to say, all the deep-down-gut-inspired fullness of who your characters are and what they want onto the page. No censuring.

That's what this chapter will help you do: put your stamp as a writer into your story. In essence, you will be putting all the emotion, all the stuff you really want to say, all the deep-down-gut-inspired fullness of who your characters are and what they want onto the page. No censuring. No editing. No self-judgment. That's why I call this the WTF Draft. (For those of you who don't text, I'll let you figure out what the F stands for: "What the _____.") And, yes, it also stands for "Write the Feelings."

PUTTING THE HEART AND SOUL INTO YOUR NOVEL

Just as the Sketch Draft is the bare bones framework of your novel, the WTF Draft is everything else: the emotion, description, internal dialogue, metaphor, simile. This draft contains all the emotion you want to convey in your scene. In this draft—which is actually a *completely separate draft* from your Sketch Draft—you will pour out the *effect* you want each scene to have on your reader: the fear you want to convey in a ghost story, the anger from a betrayal, the heartbreak of a loss, the embarrassment of being caught in a lie, the wonder of a discovery, the flush of new love.

The WTF Draft is: the emotion, description, internal dialogue, metaphor, simile. This draft contains all the emotion you want to convey in your scene.

So, how do we get there?

You write from each character's heart. That means getting deep down inside each character, experiencing each scene as that character does. The most effective way to do this is to write in the first person, as though the character was making a journal entry. Now, as we learned earlier, we know that each scene will be told from only one character's POV. But to get to the full richness of every scene, you need to understand where each of your characters is coming from. How are the non-POV characters experiencing the scene?

If you're a plotter you may find this step a little intimidating because who knows where it will lead you? That's the idea. This is a safe place to let your mind and emotions run rampant. Remember: You still have the structure down that you so carefully laid in place.

Pantsers, on the other hand, will most likely find this step much easier—and more joyful to do. No caveats here; just have fun.

Like the Sketch Draft, this is a three-step process. Here goes:

STEP ONE: GATHER

First, be sure that you have set aside enough time to begin this process. I find that sessions of between thirty to ninety minutes work best. Less than thirty minutes does not give you enough time to build momentum. And longer bouts than ninety minutes may give you diminishing returns. Your body and mind need a break to work optimally. Also, be sure that you won't be interrupted and that you've chosen a space in which you feel comfortable to write.

Before you start writing, gather the following:

- Your Sketch Draft

- Your Scene Stack

- A timer

- Your method of writing (computer, pad and pencil, journal, etc.)

STEP TWO: PREPARE

Starting with the first scene, read your Sketch Draft. Next, go to the corresponding Scene Card and circle the WHAT, WANT, OBSTACLE. This will be a reminder to you of *what* happens in the scene and—even more important for this process—What your character *wants* and what *obstacles* are getting in her way.

STEP THREE:
SET YOUR TIMER FOR TEN MINUTES—AND WRITE

To get your passion on the page, you need to send your left-brain analytical mind packing. The best way to do this is to write continuously in at least ten-minute stretches. That means that you will not pause to think, go back and fix a mistake or add a word, do any editing of any kind, or lift your fingers off the keyboard or pencil off the page—for at least ten minutes. You are going to write whatever comes into your mind for the character, no matter how weird it may seem to you. And if you hit a wall, you're going to write either, "I have no idea what to say next," or keep repeating yourself until the next idea comes. And it will come. Think of it as a marathon runner hitting a wall. If he keeps going and pushes past that wall, he will find his "second wind" and be able to finish the race. For writers, that "second wind" is what others see as flashes of brilliance.

This is going to be the primary way you are going to get your passion on the page. For each and every scene in your novel, you're going to write for at least ten minutes without stopping. Write everything and anything that comes to mind about what you *really* want to convey in this scene.

There's no right or wrong way to do this. Isn't that freeing? As I mentioned earlier, I find that many of my authors get the best results by writing from the first person POV of each of the major players in the scene. This allows them to connect with their characters on a very personal level.

> Many of my authors get the best results by writing from the first person POV of each of the major players in the scene. This allows them to connect with their characters on a very personal level.

Here are some things to keep in mind while writing:

Write with all the five senses: what your characters hear, see, smell, taste, touch. And then write with your sixth sense: what your characters feel, what they know deep down inside, what they fear, what they desire, what they know to be true. If you've done the work in Chapter 3, Journey to the Center of Your Characters, this should come fairly natural to you.

If the timer goes off after ten minutes and you're on a roll, just keep writing until you run out of steam.

Avoid the impulse to censure yourself, even if you feel that what you're writing is ridiculous. This is where you'll be accessing your right brain—the part of your brain that makes the connection between related as well as seemingly unrelated things, that thinks poetically instead of analytically, that reveals deep emotion.

As you write, you may find "illogical" ideas, actions, thoughts, etc., creeping into your writing. That's good. The right brain by its very nature is illogical. Besides, you've already worked out the logical stuff in your Sketch Draft. Sometimes the seemingly illogical actually signals that you are writing with originality and deep emotion. Welcome it! That's why it's called the WTF Draft.

If you find yourself going off on a tangent—provided the tangent has some connection to the story you're telling—see where that tangent will lead you. You may find something surprising or fresh. For instance, a character may suddenly remember an incident from her past that you hadn't previously known. Go with it. Maybe there's a reason she's remembering it. It just might be the information you need to explain a character's actions or fill in a plot hole. Or it may just be a tangent that doesn't add anything to the story. But you won't know unless you write it.

If you run out of ideas before the ten minutes are up, keep writing anyway. Write about how you've run out of ideas; write about how difficult you're finding this exercise; keep repeating the last words you wrote until your brain makes the leap to the next thought. This is your "second wind"—the place where your true creativity is allowed to flourish.

If you run out of ideas before the ten minutes
are up, keep writing until your brain makes
the leap to the next thought. This is your
"second wind"—the place where your
true creativity is allowed to flourish.

Each scene of your novel should have a corresponding WTF Scene. Whereas the Sketch Draft should be clear, logical, and spare, the WTF Draft should be all emotion, texture, and what lies beneath the surface. Finally, this is an unconstructed draft. Don't worry about hitting all the beats as they correspond to the Sketch Draft.

Remember the Sketch Draft of "The Best Intensions" that Brianna did in the previous chapter? The following is the same scene, written as a WTF Draft.

WTF DRAFT:
THE BEST INTENSIONS

POV John:

She looks really rundown—not like my mom. And there's definitely a smell happening. I wonder if she realizes that everyone in here seems to be leaning their bodies away from her as she passes by. It's embarrassing. And now I'm lying to her about why the kids aren't here—they're terrified, honestly. I couldn't even get them in the car when I told them where we were going. It's upsetting that they heard she's a witch, but I also get it. She looks like it, honestly—and that's the thing, I don't want to be honest with her. I want to go on forever making up excuses for why the kids aren't coming around to visit.

I don't want to break her heart, and I don't want to ask an old woman to change her ways. She loves me unconditionally, so I should, too, right? But I hate her for a lot of things: for letting herself go, for putting me in this position.

And before I can talk myself out of it, I tell her: the kids are scared of her; that's why they're not around. And she's denying it—but even the kids at the other booth won't look at her for more than a second before they're so scared they duck down and hide in their parents' coats. And the parents are looking over at me like there's something I should be doing about this entire situation.

So, I'm inviting her to their soccer game, and I'm reaching my hand across the table. Her hand is softer than I expected it to be, and it's been a long time since we've really touched.

I don't think I could live with myself if I make her cry. She has the best intentions. And now she's crying. I want to cry but instead I'm staring out the window, and suddenly, out of nowhere, this kid is slapping his palm against the glass and running through the parking lot shouting. I don't know what to say so I just look down, and Mom is wiping the table, like that will make her grandkids want to come to her house sometime this week for dinner. I don't know how to leave her, now that she knows she's so alone.

POV Eleanor:

I can't believe he's so old now, and I can't imagine what the kids must look like. I know they were in the neighborhood, and there doesn't seem any true reason why he wouldn't bring them by for a trick-or-treat. I feel like everyone in here is staring at me, but I guess I haven't been out and about in the neighborhood for a while. Or maybe I'm imagining it.

John won't really look up at me—I'm worried now, like something terrible has happened. If it's one of the grandbabies, I don't think I'll recover. I know he's lying to me—the kids were in the neighborhood; Susan told me so. They came by her house all dressed up, and I pretended when Susan told me like I'd seen them, too. It's humiliating, not seeing your own grandkids on Halloween. I don't know if John understands that. That he's embarrassed me. He's acting now like they were afraid of me or something—how ridiculous.

I've never been anything but a kind, sweet grandmother to those kids; there's no reason for them to be afraid, unless that wife of his is saying things—which I wouldn't put past her. But he's right, the kids in here are hiding from me ... And am I crazy or do the parents seem like they're mad at me just for being here? I know my hair's gotten a little long, and it's not like I go shopping for clothes much, but I hardly think—it's been such a long time since I cried in public, this is humiliation on top of humiliation. He's grabbing my hand with his, and it doesn't feel welcoming—it feels stiff. Like he's going through the motions. So, I'll just wipe down this table and tidy things up and be on my way. It's not right, to be treated like this at my age, after everything I've done for him, and for those grandbabies. The kids from the nearby table won't even look up when they run past me. It must really be true then. They're afraid. I keep cleaning. The boy smacks his hand against the glass, and I swear I can feel it touching my face—my breath is gone for a minute, so I just look down and keep tidying. That's what John seems to think I need to do, anyhow. He's hardly saying anything at all.

You get quite a different feeling reading these passages than you did with the Sketch Draft, don't you? I know I felt myself welling up with tears at this. The emotions are so raw, so honest, and I feel as if I am in the shoes of both John and Eleanor.

In writing this way, using the first person POV of each character, Brianna has given equal weight to both characters. This will help her keep a balance when she blends the two drafts together, even though the scene will be from John's POV. Unless the writer has fully explored what's going on with Eleanor, we could end up with a one-sided, rather hollow scene. I know that won't happen with this scene!

BEFORE MOVING ON

Have you immersed yourself in the emotions of all the critical characters in your scene? If you struggled to see much difference in the perspective of one character and another, you probably didn't entrench yourself deeply enough in each character. You might try writing a WTF Draft for one character, and then waiting a few hours—or even a day—before you sit down to write from the alternate perspective. The more difference exists between characters in your scene, the more material you'll be able to mine as you move forward with your writing.

AUTHOR INSIGHT

Here's what I got from the WTF Draft:

Organization. I finally understand the emotions driving my character, from the beginning when all is ordered and calm, to the messy middle when life frays at the edges of the character's ability to focus on the goal, to the climax when the feelings and issues that have been building to this moment influence her decisions when it matters most.

Conflict: The WTF Draft allowed me to get in the head of the main character and see how her emotions drive the decisions she makes as the story progresses. It also showed me where to swap narrative for feeling, which allows me to bring more life to the story as the character gives insight into the ways her thoughts and actions guide her. It also helped the character to become three-dimensional and relatable. Finally, the WTF version showed me where emotions can be a catalyst for explosive moments and original conflicts the reader wouldn't see coming, as emotional decisions are not rooted in logic, but feeling, which sometimes takes one down more creative and controversial paths.

Pacing: Finally, the WTF Draft has helped structure the pacing of my novel, shaping it into a more nuanced, surprising, and deeper piece of work.

—Jennifer Snell, author *The Cold Open*

THE WTF DRAFT: HELPFUL HINTS

- Write continuously in bursts of at least ten minutes.

- Write from the POV of each character in the scene.

- Writing in the first person helps you get beneath the surface.

- Don't worry about following the exact structure of the scene.

- Write with all five senses: sight, sound, smell, taste, and touch.

- Then write with your characters' sixth sense: what they sense, feel, and know to be true.

- Don't censure yourself. Remember: WTF!

10

PUTTING IT TOGETHER
Constructing the Working Draft

IF YOU'VE BEEN following this process along in the order I've presented it, by now you should have two entirely separate drafts:

1. The Sketch Draft

2. The WTF Draft

You're also probably itching to do some actual writing of your "real" draft. Those finer nuances will come later. Yes, I know, I keep saying, "Later, later." For now, though, we're going to create a **Working Draft**. This is where you're going to meld together your Sketch Draft and your WTF Draft. Like the two drafts before, this one also has three steps. Here's how to do it:

STEP ONE: MINE FOR GOLD

Print out your WTF Draft. Though many writers today are accustomed to reading and working on a computer or e-reader, I strongly urge you to work from "hard copy." This will allow you to flip back and forth easily and to catch things that you otherwise would miss if reading an electronic version. That's partly because your eyes don't tire as easily. Also, most readers still read books the old-fashioned way.

As you did with the Sketch Draft Test, you're going to put aside a block of time all to yourself to read through the WTF Draft uninterrupted. Read with a highlighter pen or your favorite implement to underline passages. As you read each scene, highlight those phrases or sentences that really stand out for you for one reason or another. Here's what you're looking for:

- The phrases or sentences that you know for sure you want to end up in your novel.

- Expressions that really speak to you.

- Images you find intriguing.

- Those words or phrases that seem to come out of nowhere and belong to nothing, but that you really like.

- Emotions that feel true.

- Bits of dialogue that crackle.

Here are a few elements that leapt out for Brianna in the Sketch Draft and WTF Draft of the diner scene:

- John and Eleanor's mutual embarrassment.

- The image of the child's hand smacking against the window—knocking the wind out of John and smacking across Eleanor's face.

- John's gesture: reaching his hand across the table.

- "I couldn't get them past the gate."

- "They hate me, don't they."

STEP TWO: CREATE A NEW VERSION

For each scene in your novel, have the corresponding Sketch Draft scene and highlighted WTF Draft in front of you where you can easily refer to them. Now, open up a new document on your computer. This is going to be your **Working Draft**.

Using both drafts as a guide, begin writing your Working Draft, pulling the words, phrases, bits of dialogue, action, description, internal thought, etc., as needed for the flow of the scene. Avoid the temptation to simply insert the WTF Draft material into your Sketch Draft.

Avoid the temptation to simply insert the WTF Draft material into your Sketch Draft.

When you are working on an existing draft, it's natural to become wedded to the words that are already on the page. By starting a new document, you leave yourself free to create something fresh, while still adhering to the structure and other elements you laid down.

If you get additional ideas as you write, go for it! The aim here is to make the writing process as easy and free-flowing as possible, yet to keep within the basic parameters that you set forth in your Sketch Draft.

The plotters among you will need to resist the temptation to discard ideas that don't fit with your preconceived ideas about how things should go. Open yourself to the process. Allow yourself to go in a slightly different direction if something is speaking to you strongly.

Those of you who are pantsers may be tempted to go off the rails with all the interesting things that came up in the WTF Draft. While it may be tempting to go off in an entirely new direction, be careful that you don't simply ignore all the good work you did with the Scene Stack and Sketch Draft. This is the time to exercise a little discipline into the process. Yes, I know that can be hard!

STEP THREE: KEEP MOVING FORWARD

As you write, avoid the urge to go back and reread the scene. The goal is to push through to the end of your draft. If you spend time revising what you've written, you run the risk of ending up in perpetual revision, never actually finishing your draft. Just make it to the finish line. Revision will come later.

WORKING DRAFT:
"THE BEST INTENSIONS"

John watched his mother walking through the diner, the people seated on either side of the aisle leaning away as her clothes and hair brushed against their tables. His cheeks flushed as she waved at him.

"Haven't been here in ages!" She smiled and slid into the red booth.

"Yeah." He watched his mom reading through the menu, and sipped his coffee. He knew the question was coming.

"Where are the grandbabies today?" Her eyes didn't lift from the menu as she asked.

"Soccer practice." A lie.

"I missed y'all on Halloween."

Two children in a booth a few tables away were wrestling. John turned his head just in time to see them glance at his mom and duck down behind the booth.

"We were in a different neighborhood." Another lie. "I'm thinking of ordering the pie." He felt the lie rush from his mouth and the quick cover up—like a dog burying a bone in the backyard. He pleaded in his mind: don't find it, don't find it.

Several minutes passed—not in total silence, but John didn't know what they were speaking about. Like one of those out-of-body experiences, he felt himself looking down on the table, watching himself speak with this woman, who he hardly recognized. She was, quite obviously, a crazy old woman.

"Tell me why they didn't come." She was making direct eye contact now, and John snapped back into their conversation.

"Honestly? I couldn't get them past the gate. The kids really missed you though." He didn't know if her face really changed, or if he was just projecting. He thought he saw tears starting to pool. He couldn't look at her anymore.

The children in the nearby booth were giggling and whispering the word "witch." He wasn't sure whether she could hear them, or if she could hear, whether she knew she was the subject of their ridicule.

"They hate me, don't they." She said it like a statement, not a question. So, now was the time. John could tell her that her grandkids hate her, or clue her in on what's really going on.

"They're afraid of you—of the house. I wish they weren't. The other kids told them it's haunted." The children at the neighboring booth were layering on their coats and hats, getting ready to be escorted out by their parents.

"Don't be ridiculous!" she scoffed. As if rehearsed, the children ran past their booth, heads down, as their parents walked by, shaking their heads and glancing at John's table—at his mother, he thought. She burst into tears.

"The kids have a game on Friday, if you want to come by." He shook her hand a little in his, but she wouldn't look up. As if she could fix this, she pulled away, crumpling her napkin in her other fist, and began wiping down the table.

There was a loud smack on the glass of the window, and John looked up in time to see the young boy from inside the diner, now outside running through the parking lot, screaming "Witch! Witch! Witch!" His parents, mortified, tried to capture him. Eleanor was clutching her cheek, as if the hand had reached through the window and swiped across her face. He gestured to the waitress.

This is getting very close to being a complete draft, though there are still some rough patches and clunky spots. Some of the transitions are a little awkward, and the scene is lacking in what I like to call "texture"—the beautifully turned phrase, the sharply observed detail, the kind of writing that makes a scene feel fully alive for the reader. But that's exactly as it should be. The point is, the scene feels very much in place—enough for Brianna to get in there and refine it to its fullest potential. That's what the next section of this book will be devoted to: understanding and putting in all those nuances that can make your novel sing.

AUTHOR INSIGHT

I was surprised by how easily the Working Draft seemed to write itself, after doing the prep work of the Sketch Draft and WTF Draft for my characters. That said, I had to resist the urge to edit as I was writing—to pass judgment on my sentences as I was still putting them on the page.

By giving myself a limited time to create the scene, I was forced to write without doing much reflection in the moment. It was sort of like piecing together a puzzle, by pulling elements from the drafts I'd already completed.

Ultimately, I think the Working Draft—and all the steps leading up to it—helped me produce an intriguing scene much quicker than if I'd simply sat down to write the whole thing from scratch. It's also made the prospect of refining this scene seem much less daunting, because I feel I have a solid grasp on what my scene is truly about—and how it functions.

—Brianna Flaherty

BEFORE MOVING ON

Take time to have a celebration. Do something nice for yourself, either by yourself or with others. By going through all of these steps, your novel is now in better shape than ninety percent of other manuscripts out there.

Just as you did after finishing the Sketch Draft, aim to take another break. In fact, I always insist that the authors I work with take at least two weeks off from working on their novels altogether at this stage. Allowing your brain to rest will allow you to come back to your novel refreshed and able to make further connections that will help deepen your writing in a way that you wouldn't have if you had just plowed on.

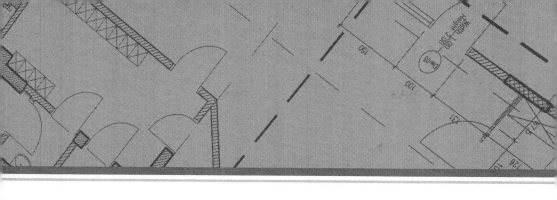

PART II

REFINING YOUR DRAFT

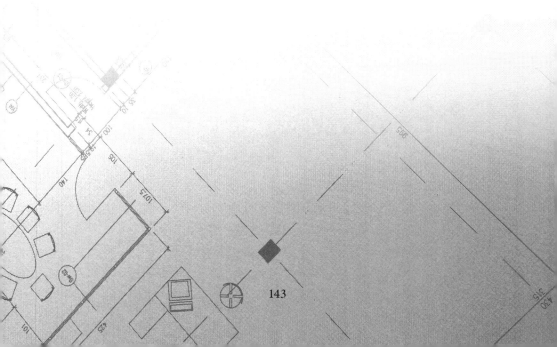

11

EXPOSITION
Making the Un-dramatic Dramatic

WHAT DO YOU do if your novel is set in a time or place that your readers will not be familiar with? Or what if you need to reveal something about a character's past that explains how and why he acts the way he does in the present? What about explaining the intricacies of how a bank vault will be breached for a heist?

All of these situations, which convey research, backstory, explanation, or a character's attitude, are known collectively as "exposition." And they are integral to helping your readers fully understand and enjoy the story you want to tell. For instance, in a work of historical fiction, details like the fabric of a court jester's garment, or the sights and smells of the streets where a nineteenth-century vendor in Florence plies his wares, can pull readers into your story—making them feel as if they are really in your characters' world. And showing just how a thief goes about cracking an "uncrackable" safe not only entertains your readers, but gives them an insider's look at a world they may know nothing about. That's part of why we read novels.

As writers, we need to be able to give backstory, to fill in the blanks, to explain why a character behaves a certain way or believes a certain thing. To give specific details of a time and place with which the reader is not familiar. To explain certain technical details that may be necessary to understanding the plot or milieu.

But here's the rub: exposition is inherently un-dramatic. By its very nature, exposition has already happened, or is merely information, which means your readers are not going to be in that exciting present moment of the story that keeps them reading.

> Here's the rub: exposition is inherently un-dramatic. By its very nature, exposition has already happened, or is merely information, which means your readers are not going to be in that exciting present moment of the story that keeps them reading.

So, what to do? Certainly, you don't want to hang your exposition out to dry like clothes on a line. You must find a way to get this vital information to your readers in a way that won't lose them.

I have seen authors write pages upon pages of exposition, with nothing happening in the present moment. One client of mine had written a wonderful, compelling novel set in 10,000 BC. It started off great—a scene from the point of view of a jackal. I was totally riveted. But then the author felt it was important to ground the reader in the history of the time and place. His instincts were right; unfortunately, his exposition went on for pages upon pages. What began as a compelling scene of a fight for survival turned into a geography book.

Eventually, the author got back to the story at hand, but by then I was out of it. I had lost interest. If I had been an agent I would have returned the manuscript largely unread.

This author's dilemma was one that many authors face—especially authors writing in a historical period: in order for readers to have a firm understanding of the time and place, they need certain details.

Historical romances, for instance, are loaded with exposition pitfalls. How do you teach your reader a history lesson just as you're getting your readers hooked? Margaret Mitchell achieved brilliant exposition by using the Civil War as a test for her characters in *Gone With the Wind*. The exposition unfolded, almost as a character itself, which impacted and changed the lives of her characters forever.

Your exposition, like Mitchell's Civil War, should have an impact on your characters. It may be much subtler, less violent and tragic, but it must affect your characters nonetheless.

If you think of exposition as one way of adding texture to your story, rather than as filling the reader in on background, that may help you approach it in the most effective way possible. Here's what I mean: Say you have a scene with a man and a woman sharing a cup of coffee. It's a new relationship, but the woman still carries a torch for her now-ex-husband. She might take a sip of the coffee and inwardly wince at the slight bitterness, recalling how her exhusband—in better times—would lovingly make her coffee each morning with just the right amount of sugar and milk. Here, the background information serves not just to inform the reader of the past, but also to show how the past insists itself upon the present. The scene now becomes infused with poignancy, which gives it texture.

Photographers refer to good exposure as the basis of a good picture. That, along with the right timing, can make a great picture. Writers, too, need the right exposure at the right moment.

What is the root of the word *exposition*? It is *expose*. Therefore, think of exposition as exposing your characters—either as memory, in a flashback scene, or in dialogue with another character. It should *not* just stand out there as a way to "fill in the reader," or it will sink your novel.

> Exposition should expose your characters. It should not just stand out there as a way to "fill in the reader," or it will sink your novel.

COMMON EXPOSITION TRAPS TO AVOID

Doing an information dump.

Imagine you're at a cocktail party and you've just been introduced to someone you've had your eye on as a possible romantic partner. You probably wouldn't start off the conversation with, "I have a terrible history with relationships. It must have started back in the sixth grade, when I had my first crush. I remember, it was a bleak November day, and Peter, the object of my crush, smashed a Yodel in my face. Ever since then, I keep thinking something terrible is going to happen." If you did, you'd probably notice the poor person's eyes darting around, looking for the Exit sign. That's backstory that probably wouldn't come out until you had your first fight and wrongfully accused him of deliberately trying to hurt you. That's when the information will actually serve a purpose: to explain your reaction to your lover.

Remember: Readers don't need to know everything all at once. That's why we read: to find out.

Readers don't need to know everything all at once. That's why we read: to find out.

Giving a history lesson.

Just because you've done an enormous amount of research on a particular subject or era doesn't mean it belongs in your novel. Your priority is telling a story, not giving a lecture. Any research that makes its way into your novel must enhance the reader's understanding of the story or the characters.

When he set out to write *Memoirs of a Geisha*, Tennessee-native Arthur Golden already held a degree in Japanese history, and he staged extensive interviews with retired geisha Mineko Iwasaki to expand his knowledge of Japanese culture. Golden would have lost many readers, though, if he spent several pages or chapters explaining everything he knew about the social and cultural structure of Japan before and after World War II. Instead, his novel ultimately became a bestseller because he never lost sight of Chiyo Sakamoto's character journey—his primary focus was always on the journey of his protagonist from poverty to wealth. His extensive knowledge and research just enhanced Chiyo's story and helped suspend reality for his readers.

Any research that makes its way into your novel must enhance the reader's understanding of the story or the characters.

Relying on dialogue to convey backstory.

Any dialogue that begins with, "Didn't I tell you this already?" or, "I guess you forgot, but ..." or, "Okay, one more time ..." or, "As you probably already know ..." is a big red flag that you are about to enter the "exposition zone." Think about it: who talks like that in real life? Unless your characters are strangers, or one character has held onto a secret, they already know the history.

Conveying information and using it immediately.

Exposition should be used to plant seeds in your story, as a way of setting up plot turns for your reader. Think of "Chekhov's gun": if you introduce a gun in the first act, it needs to go off by the fourth act. This is important not just because you need to give your reader a pay-off for anything you set up, but also because you need to *build up to that pay-off* by creating suspense. Don't tell the reader your character has a gun and have him fire it in the same sentence; let him walk around with it in his jacket pocket, feeling anxious about possessing such a powerful weapon or thinking about what he's going to do with it. If there's an appropriate delay, the reader will care more when your character finally pulls the trigger.

> Exposition should be used to plant seeds in your story, as a way of setting up plot turns for your reader.

SHARPENING YOUR EXPOSITION

Exploit your character's attitude.

Ask yourself, "What is my character's experience of the events or information that needs to be conveyed?" Good exposition holds the key to *how* your characters were affected and molded by the events. This is how exposition *exposes* your characters.

What would shatter one person might have no impact on another. Let's say sometime before a novel begins your character was in a horrible car accident. It was his fault, and another person was killed. What are some possible reactions to this past event?

"Look, if the guy was a better driver, he'd still be alive."

"Everyone has it wrong. *He* should have stopped."

"Why did I get stuck with the rap?"

"My life is over. I'll carry this with me forever."

"I was always a damn loser. Now, I'm a killer."

"I'll never get in a car again. Never!"

All of the above statements show a clear viewpoint. They do more than report a past event—they expose character. You can then reveal the backstory—the car accident in the past—as a way of explaining the character's attitude in the present.

Ask yourself, "What is my character's response or relationship to the historical detail?"

Likewise, with historical detail, ask yourself, "What is my character's response or relationship to this?" Instead of writing Tolkien-length paragraphs that talk more about your character's uniform than what it symbolically reveals about him, ask, "How does my character feel about the uniform?" Does it give him confidence? Make him feel invincible? Or does he feel like a fraud wearing the uniform? Is he having trouble bearing the weight—both metaphorically and literally—of the uniform?

Focus on word choice.

Ask yourself, "What words would my character use in referring to the piece of exposition?" Going back to the car accident example, a careless character who refuses to take responsibility for her past actions might refer to it as a "fender bender." A character who has never gotten over the accident might remember every little detail of the accident, right down to the "horrible crunching sound of metal against metal." Someone who feels guilt over the accident might refer to it as "a cross she had to bear."

Cut it to the bone.

With exposition, less is almost always more. In *The Kelso Club*, Tom Farrell lets us know a crucial piece of the main character's backstory in one sentence:

> Every gambler thinks he can run a book better than the bookie and I was no exception. The only problem was the fact it wasn't my operation, it was Zany's and now Carmine's. If I ran it into the ground, I might find myself six feet below it. They don't teach that kind of pay-for-performance in business school.

Did you catch the exposition? It was in the last line. Do we need to know which business school he went to? Or why he had gone? Or what his grades were? Or what his intervening jobs were before his present circumstances? Not really. The line says it all.

Divide up the exposition among characters.

This not only helps break up large blocks of exposition, it allows you to highlight different aspects of an event, since people remember things differently. Those differences add suspense and tension.

In *White Teeth*, Zadie Smith highlights two vastly different families—that of Samad Iqbal, an immigrant to London from Bangladesh, and the family of Englishman Archie Jones. Even in her epigraph ("what is past is prologue"), Smith announces the importance of exposition to the unfolding of her story. Each chapter focuses on a specific family and a specific person within said family.

By dividing exposition, Smith is able to succinctly establish vast cultural differences between the families at the same time that she forges human connections between them. As the novel progresses, the immense differences between characters are challenged, as their lives become more and more intertwined. So, rather than deliver a lengthy description of each family tree, and of each person's relationship to other characters in the story, Smith sets up the lives of the families and, over many pages, allows the reader to watch them slowly intersect.

> Dividing up exposition among characters not only helps break up large blocks of exposition, it highlights different aspects of an event. Those differences add suspense and tension.

Tie backstory to a current action or detail.

In my short story, "Keys," I wanted to convey how a marriage had changed over thirty years. Instead of chronicling the couple's entire history that led to them growing apart, I chose a particular moment in the present to stand in for the history. In this scene, which happens after an argument, the husband watches the wife at her vanity table performing her nightly routine:

> He sat on the bed, staring at his wife's back. He remembered how it looked when they were first married. Her hair graced her shoulders and her nightgowns were cut low, revealing the supple curves of her back. Her skin was smooth, enticing, inviting his touch. But over the years her hair had gotten shorter and the necklines of her nightgowns had gotten higher, and a rigidness crept into her back. It had become a fortress, daring him to break through.

Focus on conflict.

Instead of having one character tell another character what they already know ("How did that job interview with your former boss who fired you from your first job go?"), try to convey that information through conflict: "I can't believe you would set yourself up to get fired again from that bastard!"

"Did you break up with your girlfriend of five years, who I think is very nice?" can become, "You're not seriously throwing away five years with somebody as great as her?"

Break up the exposition on a need-to-know basis.

Exposition is like a thick, juicy steak: best enjoyed in slivers of bite-sized pieces. When you reveal it all at once, you're asking readers to stuff a bunch of facts in their heads—and then remember it all. When you withhold pieces of information, you not only create tension, but you allow it to have a stronger impact on the reader.

EXPOSITION TEST

1. Make a duplicate copy of your manuscript as it currently stands.

2. Remove every bit of research, backstory, and explanation from the scene.

Yes, I mean every bit you just put into your story! Go through each scene of your manuscript, cutting and pasting every passage of exposition into a separate document labeled "Exposition," in the order in which you removed it. Be sure to designate where it came from in your manuscript (e.g., "chapter 2, page 24, third paragraph").

3. Reread what's left of your scene.

Exposition should enhance your story world, not replace it. If without it, you're left with no action, no character insight, no advancement of story, and no conflict, then all the exposition in the world is not going to make the scene work. Ask yourself honestly if you can do without the exposition in each place that it had previously been. See if you can move exposition later, have it come out in a more dramatic way, tighten it up considerably, or use it as a way of revealing character.

4. Ask yourself, "What is this scene about?"

Is this a love scene? Is it a scene of betrayal? Is it a scene where we discover something pivotal about the opponent's motives? The story of the characters should be driving it, with exposition taking a back seat. If the point of the scene is not clear, rewrite the scene in a way that gives it life, so that it is in service of the story.

5. Cherry-pick your exposition.

Go back to your exposition-only document and choose only those details that will enhance your scene. Be ruthless. Just because you spent months researching and writing a character's backstory or the historical period doesn't mean each discovery has to make it into your book. Your readers will thank you for it.

12

ACTION
Finding Meaning in Movement

Action is critical to storytelling. Not all action, however, is a high-speed car chase, a swordfight, or a lovers' quarrel ending with someone's clothes being dumped on the street. Actions can be small, too. After all, the car chase can't happen unless someone turns the key in the ignition, the swordfight is impossible unless your character draws her sword from its sheath, and no one's clothes will wind up on the street unless somebody opens the window first. Actions, big and small, shape the path of your story. So, it's important to be selective about which actions you choose to include in your writing, and why.

> Actions, big and small, shape the path of your story.

Characters do things for strong reasons. Often, while an action may seem fairly straightforward on the surface, it's what lies *beneath* the surface of the character that gives it meaning. Too often, I see first-time authors use action as though it were just a tool to get characters from one place to another, like chess pieces on a board. But action, like dialogue, description, and internal thought, is a storytelling tool. You want to create an emotional reaction in your readers, as well as a vivid picture of what's going on. And that means choosing words that reveal what's going on with your character.

For instance, imagine your character is an exhausted middle-aged married woman bringing home some groceries. She wouldn't just bring in several bags of groceries from her car and put them down in the foyer. If you wanted to convey what was really going on behind her action you might write:

> Miriam schlepped the bags from the car and hauled them up the six steps to the house. Once inside, she dumped them on the floor, making sure she made enough of a clatter to rouse her husband from his daily nap.

What does this piece of action mean? The woman is dragging in more than the groceries; like Willy Loman and his sample case, she's dragging in her problems. Perhaps the couple has a child on drugs. Her husband deals with the problem by retreating to sleep. The wife feels all alone. By making a clatter with the groceries, she hopes to rouse him from his slumber because she can't handle the situation herself anymore. This is a cry for help. By taking this fairly simple piece of action and layering it with internal conflict and intention, we add a deep layer of texture to the action, thus heightening the dramatic tension. Additionally, the words used in this example—*schlepped, hauled, dumped, clatter*—all serve to create a vivid picture in the reader's mind.

COMMON ACTION TRAPS TO AVOID

Piling on every bit of action.

This is a particular danger in thrillers and other plot-driven stories. The writer drags the reader through every step, giving a "blow-by-blow" account of what's happening. The result is all show and no tell. We see punches being thrown, struggles, chases, knife fights, safe cracking, etc., but we don't get the *impact* of what's happening.

It can be hard to see that you're piling on too much action; after all, you have a clear image in your head of what you want to happen and want to convey that to the reader. But clear action is as much about what you *leave out* as what you put in. Imagine writing a piece of action like this:

> She quickly rose up from the chair she had been sitting in and put her right foot forward onto the floor. Very soon after that, she moved her left foot in front of the right foot. Then she repeated the same motion with her right foot. Then the left. This right-foot-left-foot motion kept up until she reached the door at the other end of the room. She stopped moving her feet and placed her right hand on the doorknob and turned it to the right, until the door unlatched, at which time she opened the door wide and went through it very fast.

Pretty ridiculous, right? This is the equivalent of writing action in super slow-mo. Our experience of action is much quicker than all the little movements it takes to perform it.

Clear action is as much about what you leave out as what you put in.

Step back, take a breath, get inside your character's head, and find ways to combine lots of smaller pieces of action into a bigger picture. Ask yourself, "What is the overall action I want to emphasize?" With the example above, you might end up with one simple line:

> She bolted from the chair and ran out of the room.

Cluttering up the action with description.

Be careful that you don't "stop to smell the roses" in the middle of some important action. This could both greatly slow down the pace and confuse readers. Here's an example of what I mean:

> She ran from her assailant, past the dilapidated apartment building, turned the too-dark corner, piled high with black garbage bags, and found herself standing in front of an old, Greco-Roman style building, supported in front by six huge columns. She stumbled and kept running.

Clearly, the reader doesn't need to know about the Greco-Roman architecture of a building as your protagonist runs past it. Though the building might be relevant later in the story, the middle of an action sequence is not the right time to introduce it as a focal point.

Ask, "What is more important to my scene: what's happening (action), or the impact of the environment on the character (description)?" If the action is more important, then leave in only those bits of description that anchor the reader in the scene.

Meaningless movement.

Too often, I see authors just detailing action as though they were simply blocking a play. Or they will have characters perform certain actions (she took a sip of bourbon; he sat down on the sofa; she crossed her legs) in a halfhearted attempt to fill out a scene. Every action should have meaning behind it. Let me repeat that: every action should have meaning behind it. So, how do you get there? Through understanding your character's attitude toward the piece of action.

Every action should have meaning behind it. So, how do you get there? Through understanding your character's attitude toward the piece of action.

Ask yourself, "What might be going through my character's mind while this is happening?" Our minds are constantly at work. It's what we think while we are engaged in doing something that truly reveals our characters.

Let's say your protagonist, a bank teller, is being robbed. The action can be direct, even a bit bland:

> The robber pointed a gun at him and shoved a burlap sack into his hand. Andrew blinked and turned to head toward the vault.

Now, let's see what happens when we infuse this action with a character's point of view:

> *This isn't happening*, he thought. The gun was pointed directly between Andrew's eyes, and the robber was shoving a burlap sack into his hand with his free arm. He

couldn't hear anything around him. The robber's mouth moved, but Andrew could only feel the blood pumping through his arms and legs. His feet were cinderblocks. His hand clasped the burlap, and he blinked. He turned toward the vault.

Through the inclusion of personal perspective and internal thought, we learn immediately that Andrew is in denial—even shock—about the circumstance he's in. We are aware of his disbelief, at the same time that it is juxtaposed with the reality of the gun pointed at his face. The other details—the loss of hearing, his pumping blood, the weight of his feet—all force the reader to experience the moment in the same slow-motion way that Andrew is interpreting the actions around him.

Interrupting the action with internal thought.

Okay, I know I just said you need to capitalize on your character's attitude with action. But a character's internal thoughts can also *intrude* on the action, slowing down the pacing considerably. Ask yourself if the thought helps move the scene forward, or if it stalls it. Does the thought clarify the action, or is it an intrusion?

Let's try a different version of Andrew's bank robbery experience:

> *This isn't happening*, he thought. *I just got to work.* The gun was pointed directly between his eyes, and the robber was shoving a burlap sack into his hand. He realized he couldn't hear anything around him. *What am I supposed to do? Should I call the police? Are there really bullets in the gun?* The robber's mouth moved, but Andrew could only feel the blood pumping through his arms and legs. His feet were cinderblocks. *I don't*

think I can move. His hand clasped the burlap, and he blinked. *I can't believe I'm about to aid in a robbery.*

The extra internal thought gives the reader the same information as the previous passage—that Andrew is in denial, scared, and uncertain. But in a scene that is clearly supposed to feel suspenseful and action-packed, these additional thoughts work *against* the pace of the action.

Unless you're giving your reader *additional* insights into your character's state of mind or the action of the scene, internal thought is likely slowing down the pace of your writing—and lessening the suspense of your plot.

In a scene that is supposed to feel suspenseful and action-packed, too much internal thought can work against the pace of the action.

Repetitive sentence structure.

Beware of action sequences made up almost entirely of the subject-verb structure. This can be wearying for readers. Here's an example of what I mean:

> He tumbled down the stairs and grabbed the metal rail. He steadied himself and ran. When he got outside he collapsed. After a minute, he stood back up. He reached inside his pocket for his cell phone and called the police.

Think of the sentences in an action sequence like notes in a song. You want to vary it up or you'll lull your reader to sleep. If you find yourself getting into a noun-verb rut, like the example above, see how you can break up the structure by combining some sentences, making shorter sentences, or switching up the order of clauses.

SHARPENING YOUR ACTION

Take it to the extreme.

Action sequences will stick in the reader's mind when they are clear, vivid, and precise. Say you have two characters fighting over a piece of clothing on sale at a bargain basement table. You could have Character A snatch the garment from Character B's grasp. There's nothing wrong with that. But why not go further? You can have Character A snatch it from Character B's grasp, then tear the garment in half out of spite. Or you could have Character A yank the garment so hard that Character B loses her balance, hits her chin on the display table, and passes out.

Slow it down.

This does not mean piling on more details, but rather slowing down the moment by adding tension to the action. In the following example, from Matt McMahon's *The Blue Folio*, the author wanted to emphasize the importance of a moment when a defendant threatens to derail the case:

> "Don't answer that," Bill commanded in a shrill voice as he vainly tried to stand. His seat was too far under the counsel table. When he tried to stand, his belly hit the edge of the table, causing him to flop back into his seat. By the time he pushed his seat back enough to allow himself to stand, Beth had already spoken, and Paul was on his feet voicing his objection.

By slowing down the moment with the action of having Bill unable to rise to make his objection, the author signals to the reader that this is an important moment and shows through the action how Bill is losing ground in the case.

Slowing down the action can add more tension to an important moment.

Sharpen your word choice.

Avoid using generic verbs. She sat down. ...He went over to the door. ...She walked across the room. ...He put his foot on the brake. ...Am I boring you to death yet? Readers need to envision what your characters are doing, and to do that, they need sharp, vivid, and specific verbs. Verbs like darted, thrust, trudged, skittered, pounced, slammed, etc., all evoke particular imagery.

Circle every single verb in your description. Ask, "Does this word convey the movement in the way I see it? Can I come up with a stronger verb that captures the movement more effectively?" Don't be afraid to think big. If you're stuck, don't be afraid to consult a thesaurus or synonym finder.

Think white space.

Action sequences work best when you break them up into shorter paragraphs. This allows the impact of each beat of action to register with your readers. And don't be afraid to have one-word paragraphs.

Action sequences work best when you break them up into shorter paragraphs.

Don't be afraid of sentence fragments.

Inserting a few fragments here and there will help keep the pacing of the action high. Fragments also serve to add tension to the scene. For example:

> She held her breath as she stared into the dark woods, listening for any movement. A twig snapping to her right. He was closer than she'd thought. Another snap. Her heart thudded as she weighed whether or not she could outrun her assailant.

ACTION TEST

Choose a scene. Highlight all the action sequences. Ask yourself:

- How does this action move the story forward?
- Does the action convey enough tension or conflict?
- Does my word choice create a clear picture in the reader's mind?
- Does the action reflect my character's state of mind?
- Does the rhythm of the sentences reflect the kind of action?
- Can I cut more words out of the sequence and still have it work?

13

DESCRIPTION
Creating a Movie of the Mind

ALL AUTHORS ARE conjurers. Using the raw materials of words, we create out of nothing a time and place. We invent a future, recreate a past, summon a present. If we're doing our jobs right, our readers will actually see in their mind's eye what it is we would like them to see.

Yet many first-time authors struggle with their descriptions, not knowing how to use description as a true story-telling tool. What you need to realize is that description is a tool to help your readers film a movie in their minds. They need to be able to see what your characters see, to experience the world of your characters through all the senses. When that happens, you transport your readers into the world you have created.

Good description is much more than window dressing. It is actually a window into a character's life and an opening to invite readers into the world of your characters. For many writers, description is also a kind of fingerprint: compare the sparing, almost terse descriptions of Hemingway to the lush, seemingly endless descriptions of Dickens.

> Good description is much more than window dressing. It is actually a window into a character's life and an opening to invite readers into the world of your characters.

On the first page of *Bleak House*, Dickens describes the muddiness of the streets, "as if the waters had but newly retired from the face of the earth, and it would not be wonderful to meet a Megalosaurus, forty feet long or so, waddling like an elephantine lizard up Holborn Hill."

Meanwhile, in *A Moveable Feast*, Hemingway's writing flourishes in the absence of extensive description, as his characters simply "ate well and cheaply and drank well and cheaply and slept well and warm together and loved each other."

There's no confusing one with the other. And one is not necessarily better than the other. But both clearly paint a picture for the reader and invite the reader into the world of the story.

COMMON DESCRIPTION TRAPS TO AVOID

Piling on the details.

Just as with action sequences, you don't need every single detail of description to evoke a clear picture in the reader's mind. A few telling details can go further than a plethora of ordinary ones. For instance, if you wanted to describe an ostentatious foyer, you might just have a character notice the crystal chandelier meant for a ballroom. That says it all, doesn't it?

Here's an example of a passage that piles on the details:

> The office was dark, and stuffed with two large couches and an expansive, oak desk. The wall behind the desk was lined with books, none of which seemed to have been touched in years. A glass that must, at one point, have had water in it rested empty next to one of the couches.

The reality is that you can give your reader the same vivid image with fewer details:

> The office was dark, stuffed with a large desk and hundreds of books. Everything was covered in a thick layer of dust.

Failure to engage the senses.

The first impulse in writing description is to go with what something looks like. But as a writer, you need to push further to help your readers inhabit your scenes, just as your characters do. People experience the world using all five senses. For instance, instead of simply describing how a dilapidated room *looks*, bring in the *smell* of mold and dust and stale cigarettes, the *sound* of the creaking floorboards, the *feel* of the grimy surfaces, and the sour *taste* of decay.

Don't be afraid to mix it up with the senses either. For instance, a character could describe the cold air as shrill (hearing), or as reminding her of lemon ice (taste). A sweltering day could be described as fetid (smell).

Not integrating description into the scene.

Description is not a time-out to create a picture. Like exposition, it must shine a light on your story. Yet many first-time authors get caught up in writing description as a separate entity—something that gets appended onto a scene rather than a tool to deepen a reader's involvement with a scene. Consequently, they end up sounding like a real estate agent trying to sell a house. The best description builds tension and illuminates character. It makes a scene come alive so that the reader feels *a part of* the scene rather than *apart from* the scene.

> Use description to build tension and illuminate character—make a scene come alive so that the reader feels a part of the scene rather than apart from the scene.

See if you can delay describing something until a character interacts with the object or setting. If your character is staying in an unfamiliar, high-end hotel and feels totally out of her element, instead of describing the entire room when she enters, hold off on the details until she must interact with them. Show her frustration in not being able to figure out the high-tech system for raising and lowering the shades, or her mounting panic as she attempts to get the overhead shower to turn on without getting blasted with water from all the other fancy jets.

Not capitalizing on the character's attitude.

Description in and of itself is boring. What characters choose to notice—and their attitude toward what they notice—is revealing.

For instance, say you have a scene that takes place in a small, cluttered apartment. A character who spent the first few years of a happy marriage there might describe the "cozy nook where she and her husband enjoyed lazy Sunday mornings with the newspaper and a cup of freshly brewed coffee."

Description in and of itself is boring. What characters choose to notice—and their attitude toward what they notice—is revealing.

But what if that character was leaving a marriage? She might describe the apartment like this: "The overstuffed furniture and towers of books and silly objects insisted themselves onto her, begging for her attention." The description gives us a sense, not just of what the place looks like, but of how it makes her feel, and clues us in to why she might be ending the relationship: an overly needy husband.

Or what if your character came from an upper-middle-class background, and was now forced to live in reduced circumstances: "The place was a dump, too confined for any normal-sized person with any ambition to live. What was that odor wafting up from the first floor? Cabbage soup? Repulsive."

Not matching word choice to the character.

Keep in mind that description should always reflect the attitude and experience of the POV character of the scene. Here's an example of the same setting, but seen through the eyes of two vastly different characters:

> The scent of lilacs floated through the air. The room was pristine, peaceful, and filled with endless rows of books,

an invitation to escape for hours at a time. A picture window opened a vista to the ocean. Could one imagine a space more conducive to relaxation?

VS.

The place stunk of dead flowers, but he couldn't see any lying around. The room was too damn quiet, too clean, and too stuffed with books. It wouldn't be possible to read this much in a lifetime, not with the constant crashing of waves outside the ridiculously large window. The room put him on edge and he wished for escape.

Notice how the word choice clearly delineates each character: "the scent of lilacs" versus "stunk of dead flowers," "peaceful" versus "too damn quiet," and so on. There's clearly no mistaking one character for the other.

SHARPENING YOUR DESCRIPTION

Go for power words.

Take every vague word and switch it out with a more extreme version. For instance:

Pretty = gorgeous

Small = tiny

Tall = towering

Loud = ear shattering

Cold = frigid

Instead of this:

He was a short, fat man, who always looked tired.

Try this:

He was a squat, portly man, who always looked exhausted.

Use metaphor or simile.

Metaphor and simile can convey in just a few words what would otherwise take a paragraph to describe.

Instead of this:

More than anything, she wished she had better memories with her deceased uncle, but time had passed by so quickly when he was still alive.

Try this:

More than anything, she wished she had better memories with her deceased uncle, but time is a thief.

One caveat: Be judicious with your use of metaphor and similes; otherwise, they can call attention to the *writing* rather than the *story*.

Substitute active verbs for passive language.

Passive language (any form of the verb "to be") not only drags down the pacing of a scene, but also makes it harder for readers to see what you have in your mind. When you use active verbs, readers have a much easier time forming a picture in their minds. Consequently, they're more involved in the scene.

Instead of this:

> There was a green vase on the windowsill. The blinds were pulled up nearly all the way. The sun was streaming in brightly.

Try this:

> A green vase teetered on the edge of the windowsill. Someone had yanked the blinds up nearly all the way, allowing the sun to pierce the room.

Play with opposites.

Using unexpected comparisons forces the brain to create indelible images. See how Tana French pairs the image of fire when describing water drops in *The Likeness*:

> He shook water off the leaf: droplets flying, bright as fire in the crisscrossing sunbeams.

Using this technique, you can go from this:

> The large, mangy dog meandered down the sidewalk.

To this:

> The large, mangy dog delicately navigated the pavement.

The reader's image of this dog now becomes much more specific because the mind has to reconcile "mangy" with "delicate." We now have a much more specific image of the dog. However, the same caveat as with metaphor and simile holds true with opposites: use sparingly. Like a good imported olive oil, a little goes a long way.

Capitalize on your character's emotional state.

For instance, in Matt McMahon's *The Blue Folio*, set in the not-too-distant future, the main character, the counsel to the President of the United States, feels tarnished by what he has been asked to do to defend his client. At a low point, he finds himself in the Lincoln Sitting Room of the White House and describes it this way:

> The most prestigious living room in the world and it looked like a pigsty. Furniture covered with sheets, piled with papers and communication pads. Coffee cups and glasses, all more than half empty, littered every level surface.
>
> There was a time when he viewed the White House as a different world. A world of class and prestige. Sitting alone on the couch, he didn't feel classy or prestigious. It felt like he had just woken up in a cheap motel room after a raunchy bachelor party.

The words that McMahon uses to describe the setting—*pigsty, littered, cheap motel room, raunchy bachelor party*—clearly show a character feeling disgusted with himself.

DESCRIPTION TEST

1. Make a duplicate copy of your manuscript as is.

2. Choose a scene and copy and paste all the passages of description into a separate document.

This will allow you to analyze how you've handled the description without getting distracted from all the other storytelling techniques. Ask yourself:

- **Do I need as much description as I have?** If a passage of description goes on for more than a paragraph, see where you can break it up and mete it out throughout the scene.

- **Are my word choices as sharp as they could be?** Remember: You want something specific to come to mind with your readers. The color red can be substituted with crimson, or ruby, or scarlet. Each "red" conjures up a very different image.

- **Can I create a more vivid picture by combining smaller pieces into a larger whole?** Think of the overall effect you want to create. Can one, telling detail stand in for all the others?

- **Does the description reflect the mood of the scene or emotional state of the POV character?**

- **Have I duplicated description?** Once you've isolated the description, it will be easy to see where you might have described something one too many times.

14

DIALOGUE
Speaking on Purpose

A NY NOVELIST CAN tell you how difficult it can be to create a passage of dialogue that sings. A brilliantly written conversation between two or more of your novel's characters can drive your novel forward, develop a character, or entertain or invite readers to understand your story world in a deeper way. On the other hand, a flat interaction can cause your reader's mind to wander off like a lost puppy.

Dialogue is one of those fiction techniques that either come naturally or don't. Some authors can easily write pages upon pages of dialogue, while others cringe at the idea of having their characters actually speak. I used to fall into the latter category. I remember the very first short story I wrote—I was so terrified of dialogue that I managed to write the entire story without one word being uttered by any character. That was quite a feat! Later, after learning a little more about how to use dialogue, I went back into that story and layered in some exchanges. And after that, I even went on to write some screenplays. Try writing one of those without dialogue. Once I broke the ice, I found that there's nothing to fear from dialogue—if you understand how to use it and what pitfalls to avoid.

COMMON DIALOGUE TRAPS TO AVOID

Dialogue that goes on for pages and pages.

A novel is not a play. Readers need to visualize what they're reading. When you go on for nearly a page or more with nothing but dialogue, readers get lost. They need something to anchor themselves in the scene.

To remedy this, intersperse your dialogue with action, description, and internal thought.

> When you go on for nearly a page or more with nothing but dialogue, readers get lost. They need something to anchor themselves in the scene.

Wordy exchanges.

Unless your character is a motor mouth, keep to one or two sentences with each exchange.

A simpler conversation is not only more believable, but also helps to keep the pace moving in your novel. By keeping your dialogue tightly focused on its most important points, you'll find it's sharper.

The key is to really boil down to the conversation's most important points. Ask yourself, "What is the purpose of this exchange? What is the most crucial piece of information that readers should walk away with?" Try keeping each exchange between one and ten words. See if that sharpens and livens up your characters' conversation.

Unnatural dialogue.

"Stilted dialogue" is one of my most frequent margin notes. Either the writer is using words that are more common to written than to spoken language ("however," versus "but"), or the dialogue is written in complete, grammatically correct sentences ("I plan to go to the grocery store later this afternoon. Do you want to accompany me?" versus, "I'm going to the store later. Wanna come?"). Most people don't naturally speak in complete, grammatically correct sentences. Well, maybe college professors and copy editors do, but the rest of us speak in fragments, run-ons, and slang. Unless your character purposefully speaks properly to prove a point or to elevate her image, strive for more realistic speech.

> To help tune your ear to natural speech, record random bits of conversation you have with people throughout your day, using a recording app on your smartphone, or some other device.

To help tune your ear to natural speech, record random bits of conversation you have with people throughout your day, using a recording app on your smartphone, or some other device. Listen back and transcribe. See if you can get the diction and syntax. What words do people naturally misuse or leave out? How often do people interrupt each other? See what you can apply to your own characters. This technique has worked wonders with many of the writers I've worked with.

Flaccid dialogue.

"Hi, Mary, it's nice to see you," John said.

"It's nice to see you, too, John," Mary replied.

"How's the new job going?"

"Not bad. My boss is kind of difficult to work for, though."

"I've heard Mr. Babcock can be a tough task master," Mary said.

The above exchange tells us nothing about the characters, does not advance the plot, and can put the reader to sleep faster than a dose of Ambien.

Dialogue must have a purpose, pull the reader in, sound like someone really speaking, and reveal the characters while telling us something about their relationship. Make your dialogue be about something. Contrast the above example with this exchange:

"Mary! I wasn't expecting to see your lovely face around these parts," John said.

"Always the flatterer," Mary said. "I miss that. I might as well be invisible since you left. So, are the pastures still greener?"

"Green, ha! Sometimes I feel like the pasture—being chewed up and swallowed on a daily basis by that bull Babcock."

"So, the rumors are true, huh?" Mary said. She sidled up to John, so close he could feel her breath. "Who's sorry he left now?"

The above exchange involves the reader in what's happening between John and Mary. We wonder about their history, and we see the spark of a budding relationship or a rekindling of a past relationship. The *not knowing* is what keeps us reading and involved in the narrative.

Characters who all sound the same.

Each character must have his or her particular style of speaking, thinking, and seeing the world. People talk differently. Some speak in meandering sentences; others speak in short, choppy sentences. Some use more formal language; others use the language of the street. Even people who have the same background and education level speak differently. We have our own lexicon, our own way of speaking that puts a stamp on our personality.

The diction of each character should be so individual that a reader would know exactly who was speaking/thinking without being told.

In other words, the diction of each character should be so individual that a reader would know exactly who was speaking/thinking without being told. Rhythms of speech, length of sentences, word choice, even the order of words in a sentence all contribute to creating individual characters.

Marking time.

"Hi, how are you?"

"Okay. How are you?"

"Well, not so great, actually."

"Why? What happened?"

"My house burned down yesterday."

Dialogue like this will make readers grit their teeth. Instead, get right to the point:

"What's wrong, Jerry? You look awful."

"My house burned down yesterday."

Relying on fancy dialogue tags.

There's nothing wrong with *he said* and *she said*. It does the trick and does not distract from the dialogue. But many first-time authors get into the trap of wanting to make their dialogue more interesting, so they slap on such tags as *he grimaced* or *she smirked*. Try grimacing a piece of dialogue. Impossible, right? Equally bad is putting an adverb after said: *he said, fiercely,* or *she said, sorrowfully.* If you have to write tags like this, it means your dialogue is weak.

> There's nothing wrong with *he said* and *she said*. It does the trick and does not distract from the dialogue.

Writing with an accent.

See how long it takes you to decipher this exchange:

"Mornin, Miss Genevieve. I'm fixin' to giddy-up inna town 'round 'bout noon. Innerested in joinin'?"

"I zuppose zo, eef you do not mind ze company."

Sure, Mark Twain wrote deep dialect with *Huckleberry Finn*, but most authors cannot pull that off without making readers stop to try to sound out the words. It just takes them right out of the story.

If your character speaks with an accent, you can capture it through syntax rather than through word pronunciation. Here's the same exchange as above, but using syntax:

> "Morning, Miss Geneveive. I'm riding into town around noon—reckon I was wondering if you'd like to join?"
>
> "Merci, oui! Yes, if you do not mind the company."

SHARPENING YOUR DIALOGUE

Create clashing agendas.

Dialogue is much more interesting when characters are at cross-purposes. Then, instead of having your characters simply "discuss" something, they can debate, argue, or try to convince the other to act in a certain way. It can also add tension to a scene if readers know that one character is trying to manipulate the conversation in his favor.

For each exchange of dialogue, ask yourself, "What does each character want in this scene? What words is he/she using to subtly—or not so subtly—get what he/she wants?"

Stop! Don't answer that question.

Dialogue that misdirects, that obfuscates, that distracts, can reveal a lot about a character's motives, secrets, or hidden agendas. Also, if you have a question answered right away, it can destroy any momentum.

Resist conversations like:

> "Woah! What's that weird thing over there?" He paused, suddenly still. "I think it's coming closer!" Tommy yelped.
>
> "It's a gecko," Ralph replied.

Any suspense readers felt during Tommy's yelp immediately vanishes with Ralph's easy answer.

Find any passage of dialogue in which any reader asks a question, and find out how many ways you can have the other character avoid answering it.

Reveal character.

The words a character chooses to use should reveal her whole backstory—where she's from, how well educated she is, her social standing, her attitude, and what she thinks about. A working class character might describe a McMansion as "impressive," while someone from old money might describe it as "garish" or "nouveau."

Choose a setting in your novel. Have each of your characters give a tour of the setting using words that reveal that character's particular attitude and background.

Exploit point of view.

Capitalizing on your character's viewpoint along with dialogue adds richness and texture to the scene. It also allows you to sharpen character development.

Revealing POV through dialogue doesn't have to be limited to a character's thoughts. *How* a character says something also reveals his POV: is he sarcastic, timid, boastful, gentle? Does he use words as a weapon, a defense, to soothe, to convince?

> ## Capitalizing on your character's viewpoint along with dialogue adds richness and texture to the scene. It also allows you to sharpen character development.

Finally, you can also insert pieces of action that reveal what's really going on in a character's head. For instance, let's say your POV character is on the phone with a co-worker she can't stand. The co-worker is haranguing her about a project that's nearing deadline. Your POV character can be very polite in her response. But while she's talking to the hated co-worker, she's doodling on a notepad. What she draws can reveal her true feelings in a way that would feel too "on the nose" with dialogue.

Once you truly grasp what it takes to make your novel's dialogue sing, you may find it's one of the most enjoyable parts of writing.

DIALOGUE TEST

Do all your characters have their own way of speaking? Or do they all sound the same? One way to see whether your characters are indeed as individual as you think they are is to compare sample strings of dialogue and internal thought within close proximity of each other.

Step 1: Choose characters who have the same background or age as each other and list them on a blank page. For instance, if you are writing a cold war spy thriller, you would list the Soviets on one page, then the Americans on another. Another story might group the lawyers on one page, the detectives on another, and the criminals on still another.

Step 2: Cut and paste random lines of dialogue from each character and place them next to that character's name.

Step 3: Ask yourself, "Can I tell the characters apart from each other? Or do they all have the same way of speaking?" Even characters of the same background and education level will have different patterns and word choices.

Step 4: Adjust each character's dialogue to reflect their particular personality. Then go back into your manuscript and revise accordingly.

15

INTERNAL THOUGHT
Exploring Your Characters' Inner Lives

*Question: **What can a novel do far better than a movie?***
*Answer: **It can bring us into the inner workings of the characters' minds.***

I N A MOVIE, basically all the work is done for the viewer. The
actors have internalized the characters' motivations, conflicts,
desires, etc., and through their performances—along with the
help of the directing, editing, and music score—the viewer is
delivered a nicely packaged portrayal of each character's journey.
All you have to do is sit back and enjoy the show. You may be
engaged in the movie and want to discuss all the nuances and
meanings and character choices afterward, but essentially, you
are a passive viewer.

A novel, on the other hand, forces you to become actively

engaged with the characters. And one of the best ways the novelist does this is through internal thought.

In a movie, the actors bring nuance to the scene. In *Ocean's Eleven*, for instance, we know by the way that Julia Roberts looks at George Clooney over the dinner table that she has been hurt too many times by him in the past, doesn't trust him, is angry, and wishes he would leave. That's the skill of the actor. As a novelist, you don't have the luxury of having an A-list actor do the work for you. So, what do you use? Internal thought.

Internal thought is what is going on in the mind of the character that either gives a fuller picture of what's going on in a scene or is at odds with what the character is saying or doing. We see how the character views the other characters around her, we learn what she really believes, what her real fears are, what motivates her, what prevents her from doing something, what compels her to do something. It's really why we read novels: to dig beneath the surface.

> Internal thought is what is going on in the mind of the character that either gives a fuller picture of what's going on in a scene or is at odds with what the character is saying or doing.

Without internal thought, all we have are what the characters say and do. But people rarely say what they really mean or act without conscious thought. It's the internal thought that actually makes a scene feel real to readers, that brings it to life.

For instance, take the simple act of a character walking up a dark staircase. If you're writing a ghost story, it's not enough to have eerie sounds or strange shadows. You want to show how your character reacts inside to these external stimuli. Is she terrified? Or is she angry that a ghost would dare to invade her home? Is she trying to steel herself for a battle to the death with an evil entity? Or is she drawn to find out more to satisfy her curiosity? Only her thoughts will give the bigger picture.

COMMON INTERNAL THOUGHT TRAPS TO AVOID

Poor balance of internal thought.

It's not always easy to know how much internal thought to use. Sometimes the genre itself will help dictate the balance for you. If you're writing an action/adventure or spy story, chances are you won't rely very heavily on internal thought to tell your story. On the other hand, if you're writing a novel about love and loss, your story will most likely be told largely through internal thought. You'll need to ask yourself two questions when deciding on the balance: 1) Is there enough internal thought for the reader to fully grasp what I'm trying to convey in this scene? 2) Does the internal thought drag the pace of the scene down?

Overuse of direct thought.

Direct thought is internal thought written in the first person and is meant to evoke true internal dialogue. A character who thinks, *Wow! I didn't see that coming*, is expressing direct thought. Direct thought is more immediate than indirect and gives the flavor for a character's diction. That same thought if expressed *indirectly* might read, "He was completely blindsided."

> ## If your novel is written in the third person, direct thought should be used very sparingly. Otherwise, it calls attention to the character's thoughts and pulls the reader out of the story.

If your novel is written in the third person, direct thought should be used very sparingly. Otherwise, it interrupts the flow of the narrative and calls attention to the character's thoughts in a way that pulls the reader out of the story. You know how irritating it can be to be in the presence of someone who blurts out everything that's in her head? That's the same effect too much direct thought has on the reader. We want the character to shut up. It just feels intrusive.

On the other hand, indirect thought, which is written in the third person, feels natural. We know what the character is thinking and how she is responding, but it's more integrated into the narrative.

Long, grammatically correct sentences in direct thought.

If you're going to use direct thought, it must simulate dialogue. Think of how your own mind works: you don't actually think in complete sentences. Likewise, you wouldn't have a character think, *I can see by his eyes that he's lying to me, just as he has so many times in the past. Why did I let myself trust him?* That just doesn't feel realistic. Instead, your character might think, *He's lying! Again. I'm such an idiot.*

Redundant tags.

It should be clear to your reader that your character is thinking something. Therefore, you rarely need to cue the reader by saying "she thought." If you're using direct thought, simply put it in italics.

And avoid at all costs using the phrase, "she thought to herself." Who else would she be thinking to?

Head hopping.

Keep to the internal thought of your scene's POV character. Avoid jumping into other characters' thoughts.

Repeating what a character has already said or done.

The role of internal thought is to reveal something new or surprising to the reader. That means that if a character is thinking what is already made clear in a moment, it's not necessary. Here's what I mean:

In an effort to get on the bus before it took off, Allison tripped over a piece of trash lying on the sidewalk. *Damn! I didn't see that piece of trash.*

Well, obviously she didn't see the trash or she wouldn't have tripped over it! If you can write the word *obviously* after any bit of internal thought, then you know you don't need it.

> # The role of internal thought is to reveal something new or surprising to the reader.

Pondering instead of advancing.

This is a particular danger in novels that are largely interior. You want to be sure that whenever a character reflects on something, it's in the service of story. To figure out if your character is guilty of this, ask yourself if what he is thinking reveals conflict, motivation, a turning point, or a revelation of character. If the answer is "none of the above," then your character may be pondering, in which case the story is not advancing.

Example (pondering):

> She stopped her writing and stared out the window, watching the deer parade by. She counted only two. She wondered what had happened to the baby deer? Had it gotten lost? Died?

Example (revealing):

> She had been struggling to get out that last chapter for—what? Hours? Days? She needed a break and found it outside her window as two deer paraded by. Only two? Where was the third one? Her relaxation was short lived as she found herself obsessing over the fate of the baby deer. Had it gotten lost? Died? No, looking out her window would not bring her peace.

SHARPENING YOUR INTERNAL THOUGHT

Have your character think opposite from what he says and does.

People don't always say what's really on their minds. If you find you have a scene in which your POV character is agreeing with another character, or telling that character something he wants to hear, you can add tension, conflict, and character insight by letting us know what's really going on in your character's head.

Example:

> "Sure, I'd be happy to take on the Walsh account," George said. *And I'd also like to have my teeth pulled out one by one with a rusty set of pliers.* What was he going to say? He was backed into a corner, and if he turned down his boss's request, he'd be the next in line to get the axe.

Internal thought is the perfect place to let the reader in on something the other characters know nothing about.

Have your character reveal a secret.

Internal thought is the perfect place to let the reader in on something the other characters know nothing about.

Example:

> "I'm not hungry," he said. She would probably leave the restaurant if he told her he'd lost almost all their money on a bet last month.

Use internal thought to call attention to an important detail.

If your characters are talking about something that you want to be sure your readers don't miss, adding a character's internal thoughts makes them take their time. In the following passage, from *Shadow Man* by Cody McFadyen, we can see the intersection of three story elements—exposition, dialogue, and internal thought—working together:

> The phone rings, is picked up. "Special Agent Bob Jenkins."
>
> "Hi, Bob. This is Smoky Barrett, from NCAVC Coord Los Angeles." The normal tone of my voice surprises me. *Hi, how are you, just watched a woman get eviscerated, what's new with you?*

"Hi, Agent Barrett. I know who you are." His voice is curi-
ous. I would be too, if our roles were reversed. "What's up?"

I sit down. Take a breath. My heartbeat feels like it's coming back down to normal. "What can you tell me about
Ronnie Barnes?"

"Barnes?" He sounds surprised. "Wow, that's an old one.
About six months or so. Killed and mutilated five women.
And I mean *mutilated*. To be honest, it was a grounder for
us. Someone noticed a smell and reported it. Cops went
into his apartment, found one of the dead women, and him
with a self-inflicted hole in the head. Case closed."

"I have news for you, Bob. It wasn't self-inflicted."

A long pause. "Do tell."

I give him a synopsis of Jack Jr. and the package he'd just
sent us. The video. When I'm done, he's quiet for a while.

"I think I've been doing this for about as long as you have,
Smoky. You ever run across anything like this before?"

"Nope."

"Me neither." He sighs. It's a sigh I find I recognize. An
acknowledgment that the monsters just continue to mu-
tate, and seem to get worse every time. "Anything I can
do?" he asks.

While this scene would have certainly been effective without
the internal thought, adding it serves two functions. First, it slows

down the dialogue so the reader gets the importance of this phone call. Dialogue by its very nature can breeze past a reader.

Second, and more importantly, the addition of Smoky's internal thoughts allows the reader to witness her experience in her gruesome line of work. Her reactions seem rather blasé, and we could take this as a jaded reaction to hearing of the extensive sadism described. But Smoky is not jaded. Far from it. She feels deeply for the victims. By including her reactions to the information being relayed to her, McFadyen ratchets up the intensity of the scene. He also includes the reader in the dread that Smoky is feeling. He's invited us to sit next to her on the roller coaster, and we willingly go along for the ride.

INTERNAL THOUGHT TEST

Choose a scene. Highlight all the internal thought. Ask yourself:

What is the purpose of this scene? Is it to reveal a secret? Show a breakup? Highlight a character's skill?

Do I have too much or too little internal thought? Eyeballing the highlighted text will let you know at a glance if the balance feels right. Don't overthink it. Go with your gut.

Does my word choice fully reflect my character? Remembering that internal thought is like dialogue, you want to make sure the character is thinking in language that's consistent with his character.

Does the internal thought reveal something surprising to the reader? If the internal thought is simply reinforcing what's already clear in the narrative, then you don't need it.

16

FLASHBACKS

Bringing the Past into the Present

U SED WISELY, FLASHBACKS can add richness, emotional resonance, and depth to your novel. They can be a way to bring in
a character's backstory, to illuminate something in the present, to
add conflict to a scene by juxtaposing the past with the present,
and to surprise the reader. However, if you use too many flashbacks, or use them in the wrong place, they can derail your story.
In fact, there are some writing teachers (and editors) who believe
that flashbacks should never be used. I don't happen to agree. I
believe the problem with flashbacks is that most novice authors
use them as a crutch rather than as a storytelling tool.

The problem with flashbacks is that most
novice authors use them as a crutch
rather than as a storytelling tool.

Some of the most poignant moments in *Extremely Loud and Incredibly Close* by Jonathan Safran Foer occur when Oskar Schell recalls memories of his father before he tragically lost him on 9/11. Without flashbacks to his past, Oskar's narration would lack much of the depth, complexity, and vulnerability that made his character, even as a nine-year-old boy, relatable and compelling to adult readers.

COMMON FLASHBACK TRAPS TO AVOID

Flashbacks that go on too long.

If readers have to go through pages and pages of backstory, they will wonder why you didn't just incorporate the flashback into the greater time frame of the novel.

Flashbacks that don't advance the story.

Think of it this way: a reader gets to know a character much like you would get to know someone you've just met. You wouldn't expect to hear about your new friend's tenth birthday unless it was somehow relevant to the present. You would, however, expect to hear about problems your friend had with an ex-girlfriend if these issues are resurfacing in his current relationship.

Creating scenes like the protagonist's tenth birthday can be very helpful for a writer in building a character's biography, but you have to be ready to let these go when it comes time to assemble your story. While character is crucial in developing the story, more than anything, a novel is driven by plot. A flashback should always serve as a tool to advance what is happening in the present.

> A flashback should always serve as a tool to advance what is happening in the present.

Abrupt transitions.

Think about when you are suddenly pulled into a memory. Memories don't arise out of nowhere; they need to be triggered by something in the present. A chance encounter on a snowy day with an ex-significant-other could prompt a memory of a ski trip taken together; the smell of lilacs could remind a character of the bouquet she presented to her mother on a long-ago Mother's Day.

Be sure there is some sort of external stimulus that pushes your character's consciousness into the past. The fact that the flashback can be so easily triggered also lets the reader know that its content is important.

Just as there needs to be a reason for your character to enter a flashback, he should be pulled back to the present for a reason as well. For instance, say your character is reliving a childhood memory in which his parents are fighting. You can have the sound of a slamming door in the present echo a slamming door at the end of the flashback scene.

The reader will understand why the character is jarred back into the present. This also helps reorient the reader to where you are in the story. Think of these triggers as bookends for your flashback that will make it come across as more organic.

> ## A flashback should be used only when there is no other effective way to get an important piece of information across.

Too many flashbacks.

A flashback should be used only when there is no other effective way to get an important piece of information across. If you use too many, it begins to feel like a cop-out storytelling device. Again, your readers will wonder why you didn't just incorporate the timeline of these flashbacks into the greater timeline of your story, or they will be confused about which timeline they should be more invested in.

Getting stuck in flashback hell.

I've actually read manuscripts where a character has a flashback and—while still in the original flashback—goes into yet another flashback. Another form of flashback hell is to forget to bring your character out of the past and back into the present scene. And never have a chapter end while a character is in the midst of a flashback.

SHARPENING YOUR FLASHBACKS

Use specific, telling details.

Be sure that your flashback isn't just a poor stepchild of an actual scene. If you're going to take the trouble to use a flashback, have it play out as vividly as your present-day scenes. In this flashback, from Dale Funk's novel *Rattlesnake Road*, a law enforcement officer waits in his vehicle for backup to arrive while investigating a gruesome murder:

> On the other side of the harvested cornfield, he spotted the silhouette of a large tractor pulling an array of discs across the open field working the soil in preparation for a planting of winter grass. The familiar sweet scent of the harvested corn delivered some solace, stimulating memories of working in the fields as a child.
>
> Drifting with the aroma, he found himself as a twelve-year-

old early in the morning at the asparagus field with his brothers, sisters and parents. He could see his father in his flannel shirt, cotton pants and worn work boots that had, in some year before he could remember, been black but were now little more than roughened soiled leather. His father, thin, with worn leathery skin from years in the sun, hunched forward, an unfiltered cigarette dangling from his mouth as he sharpened their asparagus knives in preparation for the day's cutting. The cigarette smoke lingered near Cortez's eyes causing him to blink as he waited for the ashes to fall with the movement of his father's lips.

His father looked up at him as he stood waiting for his newly sharpened knife. "You've got to be the best at what you do, whatever you do," he said, the movement of his lips finally dislodging the overdue ashes, giving Cortez a moment of jubilation as he watched them float downward and outward dispersing in the early morning breeze.

"You've got to make it better for your children. Don't end up in the fields, *Mijo.*"

Notice how Funk uses scent as a trigger into the flashback. Scent is one of the most powerful memory triggers. Funk also uses sharp, vivid detail: we can smell the corn, feel Cortez's irritation of the cigarette smoke in his eyes, really get a sense of his father.

Keep it short and sweet.

Chances are, there is only one really important point that you want to get across with your flashback. Find the key moment or revealing detail that you want to convey and center your flashback on that. Avoid giving any more information than necessary.

Make it original.

There is nothing worse than a predictable flashback, that leaves the reader underwhelmed by whatever information they've learned about your plot or characters. Even if you're revealing a clichéd character history, it needs to be delivered in a unique and original way. If you can't seem to escape the cliché, it's likely that the information you're sharing in your flashback scene could be better conveyed through simple exposition or dialogue.

When they are used correctly, flashbacks have the potential to deeply strengthen and complicate a story. The key is to tread lightly.

FLASHBACK TEST

Play Devil's Advocate with your flashbacks. You want to make sure their use is completely justified. Do you really need that flashback? Be brutally honest and ask yourself:

Can I bring the information conveyed in the flashback to the present? If your answer is yes, then get to it.

Does the flashback give the reader a deeper understanding of the character or story that they could not get otherwise? If not, get rid of it.

What is the flashback revealing about the character or story that can't be conveyed any other way? Make sure time travel is justified.

Can I bring the past into the present by having the event happen within the timeline of the novel? Why can't you just move the events in the flashback to the present tense? If you don't have a logistical reason (such as a character who is deceased in the present reality of your novel), the flashback should probably go.

17

SHOWING AND TELLING
Striking the Right Balance

ONE OF THE thorniest issues most beginning novelists have is what is meant by "show, don't tell." In fact, that is one of the most frequent comments I write in the margins of the manuscripts I'm editing. Certainly, a good novel will have a balance of showing and telling. If authors showed everything, then one novel could end up being as long as a library shelf of books, and readers would feel more like they've just completed a triathlon than reading an enjoyable story. You want to engage your readers, not exhaust them.

But what exactly do we mean by "show, don't tell?" And how do you strike the right balance?

First, understand that readers have nothing more than black words strung together on a white page to conjure up an image in their minds. When we fail to supply the reader with a specific image, the reader will have to fill in the blanks, which actually takes him out of the story. If you write, *When she returned home, she saw that they had taken down her favorite tree*, that's a form of telling. The reader is left to wonder. What kind of tree? Was it a flowering tree? An evergreen? A shade tree? How big was it? Just having those tiny little questions pulls the reader out of the story. It may only be for a fraction of a second, but if you have enough instances of this, you will lose your reader.

> ## When we fail to supply the reader with a specific image, the reader will have to fill in the blanks, which actually takes him out of the story.

Let's say you get more specific and write, *When she returned home, she saw that they had taken down the magnolia tree.* Okay, that's a little better, but you can still go further in showing the reader this specific tree, and in doing so, show why it's important to this character.

How about this:

> When she returned home, she was assaulted by the rubble of branches, twigs, and stump of what had once been the magnolia tree—her magnolia tree, the one she had posed in front of for every important occasion since she had been a scraggly eight-year-old and the tree a scraggly sapling.

Now, the reader knows: a) what kind of tree this is (magnolia); b) how old the tree is (a little younger than the narrator); c) what it means to her (the tree represents a marker of everything that was important to her. Now that it's been reduced to a pile of rubble, the narrator feels as though she is no longer important. And by the use of the word "assaulted," we can imagine her flinching from the sight. It is something threatening, injurious). That's what I mean by showing.

With the above example, as you read, you are actually filming a movie of the moment in your mind. You may picture things a little differently, but chances are you will be pretty much in synch with what the author had in mind. You don't have to fill in any blanks.

So, how do you get from telling to showing? Through word choice. When you choose the right word or phrase, you avoid being vague or clichéd. You are creating something very specific to a character, setting, time, and scene. As Anton Chekhov so memorably put it, "Don't tell me the moon is shining: show me the glint of light on the broken glass."

A few examples:

Telling:

He was a very tall man.

Showing:

You couldn't miss him in a crowd. He towered over everybody.

Telling:

She was heartbroken.

Showing:

> She lay in bed for days and couldn't even muster the strength to rub her golden retriever's belly. The dog continued to roll on his back, paws poised in the air, eyes baiting her—"aw, come on, just a little rub," they were saying, as if he could will her back to her old self.

Telling:

> He was so angry, he felt like murdering his boss.

Showing:

> He sat on his hands, fearful that if he let them loose, they just might reach out and wrap themselves around his boss's neck.

COMMON SHOWING/TELLING TRAPS TO AVOID

Use of the "to be" verb.

This is the biggest, and most common, indicator that you're showing. Look at all the examples of telling above. Each starts with, "She was," or, "He was."

Relying on "feeling" words.

Look for such words as angry, sad, upset, happy, ecstatic, melancholic, hurt, bored, etc. These are sure indications that you are telling a reader what the character is feeling, instead of showing. Making the emotions stronger ("He was livid") does not count as showing.

> ## Such words as angry, sad, upset, happy, ecstatic, melancholic, hurt, and bored are sure indications that you are telling a reader what the character is feeling, instead of showing.

Use of vague, generic nouns.

When you write "dog" I picture my overeager golden retriever. So, tell me what kind of dog you mean: a yappy Chihuahua? A lumbering basset hound? Don't tell me that he got in the car; tell me what kind of car: a 1964 Ford Galaxy, a Lincoln Navigator, a Mini-Cooper. Each of these cars conjures up a very specific image.

Showing when you should be telling.

Telling certainly has its place in storytelling. In fact, the very name suggests its importance: story*telling*. Knowing when to use it most effectively can help bridge more "on stage" scenes, as well as aid in pacing.

Think of telling as those transitional moments between scenes, the summary that gets the reader from one place or one moment to the next. It can be as short as one line ("After spending the better part of the afternoon running to the post office, bank, dry cleaners, grocery store, and gas station, she arrived to her date feeling wilted.") or span decades of time.

Here's a wonderful example from *One Hundred Years of Solitude* by Gabriel García Márquez:

> For a week, almost without speaking, they went ahead like sleepwalkers through a universe of grief, lighted only by the tenuous reflections of luminous insects, and their lungs were overwhelmed by a suffocating smell of blood.

Here we have a passage of an entire week conveyed in only one sentence. Some could argue that Márquez is actually showing here and not telling; the specificity and richness of the language would seem to support that. But this is actually a brilliant example of telling the reader that a week passed while these characters were mired in grief.

SHARPENING YOUR SHOWING SKILLS

Use all five senses.

When you engage the senses it almost becomes impossible to tell rather than show.

Be a director.

Movie director, that is. Ask yourself, "If I had to show this scene in a film, how would I film it?"

Substitute every emotional description or bit of internal thought with an action.

Telling:

> She was so mad at her sister, she wanted to hurt her back the same way she had been hurt.

Showing:

> She took a marker and made neat little x's on her sister's favorite dolls—on their cheeks, on their knees, on their lips. That would show her!

Knowing whether you are really showing a moment, a character trait, an emotion, or a picture takes time to develop. It takes diligence to keep asking yourself if your words are enough to help the reader be fully invested in your story and to keep refining and refining until there is no mistaking what you want your reader to experience. Ultimately, if you keep at it, you'll know when you've got it right.

SHOW VS. TELL TEST

1. Take a passage from your novel and copy and paste it into a separate document.

2. Highlight in yellow everything that conveys an emotion or feeling.

3. Ask yourself, "If I were an alien and didn't know what that emotion or feeling was, would I be able to figure it out based on the passage?" If not, what concrete images can you provide the alien to know what you mean?

18

ANATOMY OF A WELL-CRAFTED SCENE
All the Elements at Work

A SCENE THAT HAS undergone rigorous planning and exploration—as yours has no doubt by this point—is, in itself, an art form. Remember the scene that Brianna Flaherty wrote in Part I? She ended up with a pretty good Working Draft. Now, after refining it with the techniques from this part—exposition, action, description, dialogue, internal thought, flashback, and showing—she has rendered a beautifully crafted, emotionally resonant scene.

As you read through the scene, note her economy of language—how she reveals just enough for the reader to understand fully what's happening in this scene, as well as how skillfully she shows what's happening in her characters' minds. Finally, see how she metes out the exposition in small bites at just the right moment where it will have the greatest impact.

I have gone through and annotated each of the techniques, so you can see how she employed them in this scene. As a reference, here's the original card for this scene:

POV: JOHN

Who: John and his mother, Eleanor.

When: November 2005, just after Halloween.

Where: Local diner in a rural Georgia town.

What: John meets his mother at a diner to give her an ultimatum. They talk about why she hasn't seen her grandchildren. He asks her to move into a nursing home.

Why: To establish Eleanor's mental instability, and the distance that's grown between John and his mother and her grandchildren.

How: A tense conversation, masked by small talk.

Want: To have a better relationship with his mother and to build a relationship between her and her grandchildren.

Obstacle: John's fear of hurting her; Eleanor's denial.

THE BEST INTENSIONS
By Brianna Flaherty

John sipped his coffee and watched as the morning crowd trickled out of the diner. He checked his watch—11:00 a.m.—and began ripping his napkin into thin paper shreds.

> This action **shows** his anxiety.

There she was. Just late enough to let him hope she wouldn't show. People were leaning away from Eleanor as she made her way toward his table. John could feel the heat right in his cheeks. *She must smell.* As she slid into the booth, she gathered her long, matted hair into her palm and released it down her chest with a sigh. Her face had changed more than he expected in two months. When he'd gone by the house in August, the heat had been overwhelming. There had been so much paper and garbage piled in front of the air conditioner that the cold air couldn't circulate. He moved some things around and offered to throw the trash away ("It's not trash, dear"), but it was no use. He knew, on principle, that he couldn't go back after that, not without her commitment to move into the nursing home. It had taken her this long to agree to meet him

> Good use of **direct internal thought.** Notice how it sounds like dialogue—and how brief it is.

> The **description** of her hair, and how she interacts with it, gives us a clear picture of what she looks like. Notice we don't even need the color. This is enough for now.

> This brief **flashback** sets up the present. Notice the use of specific details to create a larger picture.

217

outside the house.

He studied her as she unwound her scarf. Her eyes were gray now, and her cheeks had sunk deeply into her face. He thought he could almost see the outlines of her teeth in the thin skin. He wondered whether she knew his agenda.

He flagged down the waitress. "An Earl Grey for her, and a refill for me." He looked at his mom as he spoke, smiling.

"Where are my grandbabies today?" She beamed, staring at him as if the girls would pop up from behind the booth any minute now to greet her. He couldn't tell the truth. He swallowed, tasting the bitter coffee residue that coated his tongue.

"Soccer practice." Simple enough.

"I missed y'all on Halloween."

And here it was: the reason he'd asked her to meet him, the setup for the big lie. How to tell her that the house was filthy, her lawn overrun, that her own grandchildren cried at the thought of visiting her. She needed to agree to the nursing home, or the kids couldn't see her anymore. The ultimatum screamed in his head.

He needed an escape.

Note the smooth **segue** back into the present.

We now get a more complete picture of what she looks like. Note how this **description** is tied to the action of unwinding the scarf.

Indirect internal thought.

Notice how short and fragmented the **dialogue** is. Here and throughout, we don't even have dialogue tags (he said, she said) because it's clear who's speaking.

Use of **sense of taste** here **shows** how difficult this moment is for him.

Use of **internal thought** to set up the conflict. We really feel the tension here.

Also note how quickly the author moves through **backstory**, and how that is tied to the moment.

He turned his head and watched as, a few booths down, two children were wrestling with each other to catch a glimpse of his mom. They were the twin boys, the little policemen from Halloween the previous weekend. One of them, he didn't know which, had tried to pull Emma's fairy wings right off her back.

"We weren't in the neighborhood," he said, still gazing over his shoulder.

The swift cover up: "I'm thinking of ordering pie." He felt like a dog burying a bone. She just nodded her head in understanding and picked up her menu.

Several minutes went by. They talked, but he was floating somewhere above the booth, looking down with curiosity on this old, unrecognizable person seated across from him. She was saying something about the house, about how she'd clean it up. *So, she knows it's filthy*, he registered. She was—and there was really no way around this when he looked at her—a crazy old woman. The gray eyes, gray hair and torn sweater weren't helping things.

From his aerial perspective he watched as the twins' parents stuffed their flailing arms

The **action** here is brief and clear. It paints a picture without slowing down the scene.

Brief bit of **exposition** tells us everything we need to know about these brats.

Action shows his evasiveness.

Use of **simile** to express his emotions.

Note the use of **figurative language** to show his emotions, which are so strong he has to dissociate himself from the scene.

Direct thought. Again, note how terse it is.

into their coats. Maybe he should've brought the girls along. Eleanor was so excited the day Emma was born, she even beat him to the hospital. Maybe seeing the girls now would snap her out of it, whatever it was. How bad could it be?

Active, vivid language.

*One brief dip into **backstory** to show the relationship Eleanor had in the past with her grandchildren.*

"Tell me why they didn't come." Her words thrust him back into the booth. He thought for a minute.

"Honestly I couldn't get them past the gate, Mom." There it was. He closed his lips and pressed his tongue hard against the roof of his mouth, waiting for her response.

*This **action** clearly portrays his tension as he waits for her response.*

She tilted her head. "Do they hate me?"

He sighed. "No, no, I don't think so. They're just afraid of the house. Somebody told them it's haunted."

"Don't be ridiculous!" Her voice was shrill.

"Mom, it's not so ridiculous, the house is trashed."

"It most certainly is not." She was shaking her head and glancing around the diner. So, she could sense it was a setup, then.

*To **avoid a POV violation,** we have John sensing—by her action—what she is thinking.*

"Look, if you'll move out, I can clean it up, the girls can come visit you in the home and—"

Witch! The word flew toward their booth as the boys marched to the exit.

> Great use of vivid verbs! We can really see this.

John swallowed his speech. Maybe her hearing wasn't good anymore. He reached for her hand across the table and shook it around in his. It was so much softer than he'd thought.

> **Indirect thought.**

> Use of sense of touch.

"They have a game on Friday. I can pick you up."

She pulled her hand away and ran it through her hair until it hit a knot.

> This brief **action shows** us what is in her mind: his hand doesn't feel welcoming; she knows he's lying, that he's just going through the motions.

There was a loud smack against the window. One of the twins pressed his face against the glass, screaming through his flattened lips,

"She's a witch!" It seemed like an hour before his father, glancing at John, yanked him away. The boy took off running through the parking lot, shouting along with his brother, "Witch! Witch! Witch!"

> The use of sound creates a beat to **stretch out this moment** and add tension to it.

Twins, John thought. A car alarm went off somewhere in the lot. He heard a heavy sob. Eleanor was clutching her cheek, as if the boy had reached through the window and swiped his hand across her face. Tears

> This **action shows** how Eleanor feels.

221

The author brings back the earlier image of Emma and the fairy wings to tie it all together.

spilled down her cheeks. <u>She looked just like Emma when her wings got ripped.</u> He didn't know what to do.

He gestured to the waitress, wanting to ask for the check, then realized they hadn't ordered yet.

AUTHOR INSIGHT

All the work leading up to writing the final scene truly paid off. It seemed counterintuitive to me that doing so much planning before writing the scene would help—not hinder—my creative process. But having the Scene Card, Emotion Draft, and Sketch Draft at my disposal allowed me to generate most of the scene's content fairly easily.

I found, then, that I had more time and energy to devote to the truly creative process of writing the final scene. The kinks had already been ironed out, so there were no major concerns about the purpose of the scene, or it's function within the plot. Instead, I got to flesh out my characters, and the narrative of the story, by using my creativity.

In the end, this step-by-step approach to writing not only expedited the process of creating the scene, but also allowed me to devote greater energy to delving into my story and characters. The final scene came about quickly, and in a more fully realized and developed way than I'd ever anticipated.

—Brianna Flaherty

BEFORE MOVING ON

Be a detective. Choose a scene from one of your favorite authors. Go through the scene line by line and annotate all the elements just as we've done with Brianna's scene. Seeing how others have successfully used all these literary tools will help you to sharpen your own skills.

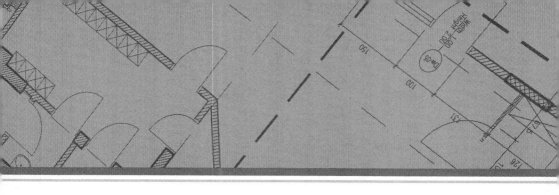

PART III

COMMITTING TO YOURSELF AS A WRITER

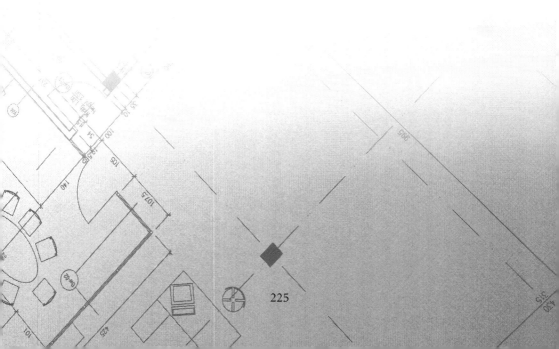

225

19

GETTING UNSTUCK

What to Do When You've Hit a Wall

"Real courage is when you know you're licked before you begin, but you begin anyway and see it through no matter what."

—Harper Lee

IT HAPPENS TO every writer: your words are flowing along smoothly, your characters are practically writing their own dialogue, your scenes are crackling. Then—WHAM! Everything comes to a screeching halt. Your characters turn mute, your scenes morph into tableaux, and English seems not to be your first—or even your second—language.

Rather than staring at the computer screen with your stomach tied in knots and cursing the writing gods, do something to break the cycle.

Your natural impulse may be to think that your ability as a writer may have flown the coop, and that your idea has dried up. But before you panic, consider this: all writers get stuck from time to time. Yes, *all*—even "brand name" writers often find themselves deep in writer's block.

All writers get stuck from time to time; even "brand name" writers often find themselves deep in writer's block.

Kurt Vonnegut even asserted that the frustration of writer's block trumps censorship: "Who is more to be pitied, a writer bound and gagged by policemen or one living in perfect freedom who has nothing more to say?"

GETTING BEYOND THE BLOCK

Whether you find yourself stuck momentarily or for weeks on end, a number of things can be contributing to your block. Most likely, any one of these culprits can be at play:

You're simply fatigued.

Writing is a strenuous task. Sure, you're not moving your legs or arms very much, but your brain is sure getting a workout.

Get up from the computer and do a few stretches, walk the dog, phone a friend, do a quick errand, empty the dishwasher, listen to lively music. It doesn't matter what you do, just do something other than writing. Activity will help clear your brain so you can come back refreshed.

If you're fatigued, it might be a signal that you're a little hungry or dehydrated. Snack on something light and healthy. Avoid anything sugary, which causes blood sugar to spike and then drop, causing your energies to drop along with it. And drink plenty of water.

Avoid the temptation to check your email, pay bills, or surf the Internet, which will only drain you more. Shifting your mindset to a physical activity, if only for a few minutes, can be the jump-start you need. Remember not to get too stressed; this is all part of the process.

Avoid the temptation to check your email, pay bills, or surf the Internet, which will only drain you more.

Your fatigue may also be a signal that you need some rest. As writers, we don't always treat ourselves well. We write in our pajamas. We forget to shower. We eat junk food because we don't want to take a break to cook a meal. The physical act of writing can take a toll, causing cramps or stiffness. Show yourself some kindness and get a facial or a massage. Get your nails done. Shoot some hoops or go for a run. A more relaxed body and mind can translate to better writing.

If you're not a fan of the spa or salons, take a nature walk, have a bubble bath, or meditate. Whatever you decide, commit yourself to finding tranquility, even for a few minutes.

Next time you feel like you've reached your writing limits for the day, remember how important it is to take a break. You might find that your writing will flow easier and that you'll generate ideas and connections you might never have thought of when you were hunched over that hot computer.

When you're writing a book-length work, it's natural to tire of your characters, story, or subject matter.

You've grown bored.

When you're writing a book-length work, it's natural to tire of your characters, story, or subject matter. After all, you've been dwelling for months on the same story elements that, ideally, a reader would digest in a matter of days. Here are some ideas you can try to shake things up:

1. **Try a different angle.** Write from the point of view of a different character, or write a letter from one of your characters to another character.

2. **Do the opposite.** Try making certain scenes come out the opposite way: if you have a murder, see what would happen if the murderer only thought he killed his target. If you have a marriage proposal, what would happen if the character making the proposal got cold feet?

3. **Exaggerate.** Take things to extremes, exaggerate character traits, have them behave in histrionic ways. In other words, have characters do what you would "never" do. You may even discover some gems worth keeping.

4. **Do a journal entry.** Sometimes it helps to simply step away from the story and write about what's getting you stuck, rather than trying to write the perfect words. Write what you want to say and perhaps

why you're having trouble saying it. The more you stay with this, the better chance you'll have of finding your way out of the rut and into something fresh and telling.

5. **Rapid write.** In this technique, also known as free-writing, you write continuously without stopping—no matter what. You either keep your hand moving across the page or your fingers typing without pausing for corrections or thoughts. If you don't know what to say, then write that or keep repeating the last thing you've written until something new comes to your mind. Do this for at least ten minutes without stopping. This will allow the right brain to take over, giving your left brain a much-needed break. When you continually write without letting the left brain interfere, then fresh, original ideas will come to the surface.

You don't have enough information.

Usually when I get stuck, it's because I don't have enough information to move forward on whatever I'm writing. Instead of struggling to find the right words, do a little research. Search the Internet, call an expert, refer to a book, or review your notes.

Rather than straining your brain to figure out what comes next, get creative. Read some travel articles or history books about your setting, or try injecting a whole new character into your story just for fun. Even if you just stick to some rapid writing, you never know what brilliant ideas may come up.

You're fearful of finishing.

Certainly, this possibility can seem counterintuitive. Why would you be fearful of completing something you have been working so hard on for months or even years? Mostly, because finishing this draft means you will be faced with getting it out into the world and facing criticism and the possibility of rejection. It means perhaps discovering that you've been wasting your time, though I strongly believe that no endeavor worth pouring your heart and soul into is ever a waste of time, even if it leads nowhere.

If you think this is what's causing you to be stuck, write about it. Write about all the terrible things that could happen when you finish your novel. Next, write about all the things you will feel if you *don't* finish. My guess is, the second possibility will be far more damaging than the first.

Despite all the obstacles, if you keep forging ahead and pushing through your blocks, you *will* finish your book—and the sense of satisfaction that will bring you will be worth all the hurdles you had to jump over.

AUTHOR INSIGHT

Here are some tricks I've developed that have been helpful in getting me over the wall:

1. Watch a *Netflix* movie of something similar to my story because I see lots of graphics and get dialogue.

2. Read a book of a completely different genre to stimulate new ways of describing things. I find that reading something different gives me new tools and empowers me a bit.

3. Do something crazy like writing down my little quotes that I know will be famous after I'm dead. (Makes me feel like I'm special and witty, ha.)

—Dale Funk, author *Rattlesnake Road*

20

AVOIDING SELF-SABOTAGE
How to Banish Limiting Beliefs

"I'm not talented enough."
"I'm wasting my time."
"It's really not that important anyway."
"I'm afraid I'll fail."

—Every Aspiring Author

DO ANY OF these statements sound like you? If so, you may be holding yourself back from success.

In my work over the years with authors of all levels, I've heard it all. Writing a book can be an overwhelming task, bringing up all sorts of uncomfortable or negative emotions. But these thoughts are just limiting beliefs—those nagging thoughts preventing us from fully committing to finishing what we started. And that's just what they are: thoughts. They are not real, just dirty tricks our minds play on us. If you give in to them, you will cut short what could have been a very satisfying writing career.

First, understand that you're in good company.

All creatives battle with these beliefs. Many writers have uttered phrases like, "Who am I to think I could write a novel?" or, "What do I have to say that hasn't already been said?" It's the writers who acknowledge these woeful beliefs for what they are—*beliefs, not truths*—who can push them aside and get back to writing their books.

Second, realize that limiting beliefs arise from the past.

Perhaps a teacher told you a story that you had slaved over was riddled with errors, or a parent dismissed your creative writing as a waste of time. Maybe a loved one felt jealous of the time you spent writing. Perhaps you never got the support you needed from a mentor or an editor.

Let's tackle each of the statements at the start of this chapter:

"I'm not talented enough."

> "It took me fifteen years to discover I had no talent for writing, but I couldn't give it up because by that time I was too famous."
>
> —ROBERT BENCHLEY

What is talent, anyway? Thomas Edison once said, "Genius is one percent inspiration, ninety-nine percent perspiration."

Even bestselling authors go through torture and feel they are not talented. With writing, the talent becomes evident through the revision process. The more you trim, rearrange, and polish your work, the better it will be. And the better chance you have to rise from the ashes of your first frustrating drafts as a better writer. It may seem tedious, but take it from an editor who has scrutinized hundreds of manuscripts, written over two hundred articles, and personally coached dozens of authors over the years—learning to push past the revision process is what transforms writers into authors. Analyzing pieces of writing for everything from the clarity of its message to the beauty of its prose has definitely made my own writing better over the years. Don't give up. Embrace your craft.

The more you trim, rearrange, and polish your work, the better it will be. And the better chance you have to rise from the ashes of your first frustrating drafts as a better writer.

And remember this: do you think you would have been given the desire to do something you have no talent for? Personally, I don't think God—or the universe—would be that cruel. What may be obvious to you can be amazing to others—as long as you aren't afraid to hold back.

"I'm wasting my time."

> "Any man who keeps working is not a failure. He may not be a great writer, but if he applies the old-fashioned virtues of hard, constant labor, he'll eventually make some kind of career for himself as a writer."
>
> —RAY BRADBURY

If you weren't writing, what else would you be doing? Watching TV? Surfing the Internet? Writing is not about how you are spending your time, but rather about how you are making the time you have meaningful to you. Writing a novel is not only about getting published. The more important questions to ask are, Am I enjoying the time I spend writing? Does it give me joy? A sense of purpose? Am I learning something about myself that I hadn't learned before? If you can answer yes to any of those questions, then you are clearly not wasting your time.

> ## Writing is not about how you are spending your time, but rather about how you are making the time you have meaningful to you.

"It's really not that important anyway."

"Writing is a dog's life, but the only life worth living."
—GUSTAVE FLAUBERT

Oh, yes it is—or you wouldn't be reading this book! The sheer act of writing is what is important. But we tend to shrug it off when our confidence begins to wane, when we're afraid that what we are writing isn't any good or that others won't give us the accolades we so desire. And, yes, everyone desires applause.

"I'm afraid I'll fail."

"Failure is just another name for much of real life: much of what we set out to accomplish ends in failure, at least in our own eyes.... Who told us we had to succeed at any cost?"

—MARGARET ATWOOD

What does "failure" mean to you? This may come as a surprise to many, but I view failure as an essential component of success. While it may seem that writing a bestseller or getting a book contract is akin to winning the lottery, I assure you that those authors who succeeded had many failures leading up to their big breaks. The difference between them and someone who allows rejection to dictate his or her reality is that they learned from their mistakes, applied what they learned to their writing, and persisted.

There's really only one way to fail: play it safe. Creativity requires risk, and risk often leads to failure—at least initially.

Perhaps my favorite rejection-to-success story is Stephen King's. We all know King's work; he's made a huge mark on literature, film, and popular culture. But did you know that he received over two dozen rejections before making it big?

There's really only one way to fail: play it safe. Creativity requires risk, and risk often leads to failure—at least initially. But what matters is what you do after your manuscript has been rejected or your critique has come back with more negatives than positives. Take it from me—don't play it safe. Strive to make your story heard, and the world may reward you.

TAKE CHARGE OF YOUR DESIRE TO WRITE

It's okay to have limiting beliefs once in a while, but if they prevent you from sticking with your writing, you need to take action to banish them for good. Here are some suggestions:

1. **Keep a pad of paper and pen next to your writing space.** Every time a negative thought pops up while you're writing, jot it down. Sometimes, just the act of writing down our limiting beliefs is enough to diminish them.

2. **Review your past to try to determine the origin of your limiting beliefs.** Was it something a parent or teacher said to you? Did you experience an early embarrassment? Ask yourself, "Are these beliefs really true? Or are these more about the other person than about me?"

3. **Take each of the negative statements you wrote on your pad and rewrite them onto separate pieces of paper.** Repeat each statement aloud. Then, burn it. (Be careful where you do this!) Watching your limiting beliefs go up in flames and turn to ashes is one of the surest ways to let them know they are no more than air. They don't exist.

21

DEALING WITH EXTERNAL FORCES
When Time and People Are Not On Your Side

"It takes a great deal of courage to stand up to your enemies, but even more to stand up to your friends."

—J. K. Rowling

AS A WRITER, it would be nice to think that all you have to do is decide to write your novel, carve out enough time to work on it, then write it. But that's the fairy tale. The reality is, the world is constantly beating at your door, demanding your attention. There's the boss who needs you to work overtime, the spouse who wants your company on your "time off," children who need help with homework, a car that breaks down and needs to be taken in to the shop, bills and paperwork that need to be attended to, friends who implore you to socialize, the "best friend" who thinks you're wasting your time and should take up golf instead.

All of these demands are a normal part of living, and for most people, they just get absorbed into their daily lives. But for the writer, it can be agonizing. You wish the world would just stop and let you write your frickin' book already. Unfortunately, the world does not wish to accommodate us writers. Instead, we have to learn how to function within it, even if it means having to say no to others and sometimes even to ourselves when other things threaten to overtake our writing.

Believe me, I know how difficult it can be. I've written six books, and each one has been a struggle against outside forces. Interestingly, the ones in which I had a hard deadline from the publisher managed to get done. No way was life getting in the way of that!

But what do you do when you don't have a publishing contract? How do you keep the momentum going and not get discouraged? My hope is that this chapter will give you some useful ideas.

MAKING TIME TO WRITE

Notice, the title of this section is *making* time to write—not *finding* time to write. And that's the key. You will never find the time. Time will always be elusive, and that which screams the loudest will command your attention. The key to fitting writing into your life is to make it a priority of your life.

The key to fitting writing into your life is to make it a priority of your life.

Let me first be clear what I mean by making writing a priority. Certainly, if you have a family or a job or someone who depends on you, those are big priorities. I'm not suggesting you ditch your normal life. And, let's face it: we all get the same twenty-four hours in a day. Nobody gets more than that. As crammed as your life may be, there are all these moments that are either wasted or spent doing things that won't help you get closer to your goal of being a published author. Following are some suggestions, which have worked for me and for the authors I've worked with.

Get up one hour earlier.

Many writers find the early morning hours to be almost magical. The sun is not yet fully up—and neither is anybody else. It's just you and your computer or notebook. Plus, your mind is not yet weighed down by the demands of the day. I know I do my best writing while I'm still "in bed," having my morning coffee and writing longhand.

Getting up a full hour earlier may be a shock to the system at first, so work up to it gradually. Wake up fifteen minutes earlier for the first week. That's not so hard, is it? You may not get a lot of writing done, but maybe you can at least write a paragraph or two before the day insists itself upon you. Then, the next week, add another fifteen minutes. Now you'll have a half hour in which to write. Keep going until you've reached an hour.

By the way, this is how I managed to fit meditation into my daily life. I kept telling myself, I don't have thirty minutes to spare! Really? But I started small, doing ten minutes at a time and very gradually working up to thirty minutes of meditation and then another thirty minutes of what Julia Cameron in *The Artist's Way* calls "morning pages" (three handwritten pages of writing whatever is on your mind with no judgment. This clears all the chatter from your brain so you can get to your writing with a clear mind). So, the hour that once seemed so overwhelming is now available to me in a way it wasn't before. And I couldn't imagine not starting my day this way.

Go to bed an hour later.

If getting up earlier makes you want to hit the snooze button, maybe you're more of a night owl. Some people do better after everyone's gone to sleep and they have nothing but the crickets to keep them company.

If Monday to Friday is just too filled with the stuff of life, carve out some time on the weekend. But make sure you're writing every weekend, or you'll lose momentum.

Put it on your to-do list.

If writing is not on your list of things you have to do, it won't get done. Why? Because you haven't made it a priority enough to put it on your list. Let's face it: how many of us actually get everything done on our to-do lists? If writing is not even on there, it's always going to be way at the bottom of the pile.

But make it easy on yourself. Do not simply put "write my novel" on your to-do list every day. That will just breed a sense of failure. Instead, chunk it down to small tasks, such as, "Write Character Blueprint for Martin," or, "Fill out the scene in the woods," or, "Tweak the dialogue in Chapter 12." These give you manageable, achievable tasks.

> Do not simply put "write my novel" on your to-do list every day. That will just breed a sense of failure.

Also consider putting all your tasks into category chunks so your list is better organized and not so overwhelming. And don't forget to list those little time-wasting tasks, such as file receipts, do the laundry, pick up milk, answer email.

Find a private place to write.

If you live with others and you're trying to write on a computer in the family room or on a laptop in the kitchen, you'll never be left in peace. Find a separate room where you can go and shut the door. Make it known that you are not to be disturbed except in the case of an emergency.

If it's not possible to do this at home, find a library to work in. Some of my authors love to write in coffee shops. Somehow, the buzz of the other customers is more like a white noise, and they feel alone in the midst of company.

I'm lucky enough to have a cottage in the woods that I rent from a friend when I need to get away to write for stretches at a time. In fact, I'm sitting here at this very minute as I type this. Even though I have my own home office, there's still too much happening at home when I want to get some real quality work done.

Carry a notebook or small digital recorder with you.

Maybe all you can really grab is five minutes here, five minutes there. Make the most of it. Write your ideas down in your notebook, or talk into your recorder or smart phone for transcribing later. But avoid multitasking. To be a good writer, you need to put your full attention on your words, not share it with driving or walking the dog or watching your kid's soccer game. Do those other things fully, with purpose. And that's really the point. When you live your life on purpose—not being a little bit here and a little bit there—you will free up all sorts of time, and space in your brain, to get your writing done.

> To be a good writer, you need to put your full attention on your words, not share it with driving or walking the dog or watching your kid's soccer game.

Learn to say no.

Do you find yourself agreeing to things you really don't want to do, or that take precious time away from your writing? It can be extremely difficult to disappoint others, and you may even feel selfish for turning down requests for all sorts of things. Let's face it: most people don't want to disappoint their loved ones, colleagues, or friends. But the more you find yourself agreeing to do things that you don't want to do, and that take up time you would otherwise spend writing, the less you'll get done and the more resentful you'll become.

Saying no does not mean you are selfish or that you are being negative or unsupportive of the other person. And you should never feel guilty for saying no. When you stand up for your needs, most people will understand.

LACK OF SUPPORT

If you're a writer who has support of your writing goals from friends and family, you're one of the lucky ones. Be sure to make them know how much you appreciate them. Sadly, many aspiring authors aren't so lucky. They don't have the encouragement of loved ones. There are those who view book writing, or the dream of becoming a published author, as a hobby instead of a true path in life. Others may be threatened by creativity. Some may even fear that you may write them into your novel in a way that puts them in a bad light. Not having the support you need from others can totally derail an aspiring author's chances at success.

Getting support from others is not just a perk—it's crucial.

Getting support from others is not just a perk—it's crucial. I know that the authors I work with who have the total support of their loved ones are the authors who will not only finish their novels, but will also do the deep work necessary to make their stories a success. This is why having support is so essential: when you get discouraged, when you feel like giving up, when you feel like you just don't have the talent, a supportive loved one or friend or colleague will be the cheerleader you need, will urge you to keep on going, will help you to see that you are not crazy for wanting to do this.

Here's how to get the support you need:

Pinpoint why writing is important to you.

Gaining a clear understanding of why you are so passionate to write—whether it is because of the thrill of putting words on a page or an ultimate dream of being published—is key to knowing what kind of support you need. It's also essential to admit and express your needs to yourself in order to avoid giving up on your dream down the road. Once you know exactly what drives you to write, and why you can't fathom living without it, you can express yourself to others in the most convincing way possible.

Gaining a clear understanding of why you
are so passionate to write is key to knowing
what kind of support you need.

Address your loved ones' concerns.

Often, when people aren't supportive, they think that your writing is going to take up their time with you. If the people you live with are not understanding, sit them down and explain how important writing is to you, and that if they give you the space and encouragement you need, you will be much happier.

Also, listen to their concerns. If you work out a plan with them so that they can be assured *their* needs are being met, you can be assured that your needs as a writer will be met. It's crucial to know you're all on the same page.

However, if you need help with certain chores that would encroach on your writing time, make your needs known. If you make the effort to sit down with your family, you'll be surprised at how quickly you'll all reach a balance.

Reach out to a new support system.

It's critical to seek out others who will support you in your writing, who will cheer you on, who will read your early drafts and give you helpful feedback. If you're fortunate to have a circle of friends who are also engaged in creative endeavors, reach out to them on a regular basis. Artists, actors, and musicians will understand the kind of support you are looking for and may even offer some fresh ideas.

Writing groups can also be a terrific source of support, though you do need to be wary of groups that can end up being more harmful than helpful. Avoid groups that have a strong competitive edge or ones in which the members seem to be pushing a strong agenda.

If there are no writing groups in your community, the Internet has made these support systems easier to find than ever before. Several wonderful online writing communities I've come to love are *She Writes, WAE Network,* and *WOW! Women on Writing. LinkedIn* has a plethora of writing groups, including groups that are devoted to particular genres. Also, the rich abundance of writing, editing, and publishing professionals I've found on *Twitter* has convinced me that no matter what your goals are, you're sure to find someone out there who shares your perspective.

22

LEARNING TO HANDLE REJECTION
And Yes, You Will Be Rejected

"Rejection slips, or form letters, however tactfully phrased, are lacerations of the soul, if not quite inventions of the devil—but there is no way around them."

—Isaac Asimov

AT THE BEGINNING of my writing retreats and workshops, the attendees each introduce themselves. On more than one occasion, a writer will reveal that he or she is coming to the class after having experienced a devastating rejection. By that I mean, not the standard rejection you get when you send your work out to get published, but the more personal kind that rips apart your writing with no constructive feedback, the kind of rejection that feels as though you are being personally attacked and that leaves you wondering if you were crazy to ever think you could write.

One of my students had entered her manuscript in a contest. As she said, "Two of the judges had really helpful critiques, but the third really ripped me to shreds. I've been having a hard time writing and revising since, wondering if I even have any talent, if I'm just wasting my time." My heart goes out this writer. I know exactly how she feels, because I've been there.

In my case, the nasty rejection came from a teacher I had revered. I can remember the moment as if it were yesterday. It was February 23, 1994, and I had been glued to the Olympics. That was the year of the infamous Tonya Harding/Nancy Kerrigan fracas, when Kerrigan got her knee whacked. In the middle of the women's short skating competition, my phone rang. To this day I don't know why I chose to answer the phone instead of continuing to watch the Olympics. But I did.

On the other end of the line was my writing teacher, who was also a well-known novelist. I had been a member of a small novel-writing workshop for over a year and had recently completed a rough draft of my novel-in-progress.

Without hesitation, she got right to the reason for her call. "I don't want you in the group anymore. You're just not getting it. I can't help you."

This was the same teacher who had once revealed to me that a story I had written made her cry because it had touched her so deeply. It was in part due to that story that she had invited me into this select group of writers. And in this particular workshop I had been submitting chapters on a regular basis and getting what I thought was helpful feedback. At no time did anyone in the group give me any indication that I was "not getting it."

I was utterly and completely devastated. I remember hanging up the phone and going back to the TV and just staring at it blankly. Nancy Kerrigan may have had her knee whacked, but I'd had my soul crushed.

I stopped writing. I became completely blocked. The worst part of it all was that I allowed another person to take away from me something that gave me joy. It was only after reading Julia Cameron's wonderful book, *The Artist's Way*, that I healed myself and began writing again.

I stopped writing. I became completely blocked. The worst part of it all was that I allowed another person to take away from me something that gave me joy.

There was one positive that came out of this whole incident, however: I vowed never ever to do to any writer who came to me for help what she had done to me.

I hope you never have to go through this, though my experience and the emotions that went with it are all too common. Anyone who has ever tried a creative endeavor has probably gone through this kind of soul-crushing rejection to one degree or another. It's the nature of the beast. If you are ever on the receiving end of this kind of rejection, here are some ways you can cope:

Step away from the emotion.

The natural response to getting a nasty rejection or a scathing review is to want to jump out a window, burn the manuscript or delete it on your hard drive, or cry into a pillow. It's okay to feel that way, and crying can be cathartic. But before you do anything more drastic, allow your emotions to calm down.

Keep it in perspective.

If you look at the quote from the writer mentioned at the beginning of this chapter, you'll see that she got helpful critiques from two judges, but it was the nasty critique that had the greatest impact on her. Don't shut out the positive or helpful responses or give too much credence to the negative ones.

> Don't shut out the positive or helpful responses or give too much credence to the negative ones.

Ask yourself what else might be going on.

Sometimes people are jealous and attack you. Others are looking to make a mark and go about it in the wrong way. Some may have suffered devastating criticism in the past and are really getting back at the person who hurt them. Still others are looking to stroke their own egos by bringing someone else down. And some just want to be Simon Cowell.

In the case of my writing teacher, I had learned from another member of the group that she did the same thing to another writer who had gotten to the end of a draft. Maybe she acted out because she herself was struggling with writing the next book she was contracted for—and the extended deadline was looming. But I moved on and was the better for it.

Read between the invectives to see if the critique has any validity.

Easier said than done, I know. But sometimes people get really ticked off over a particular thing and allow their feelings to run away with them. For instance, let's say your spelling and grammar are not up to par. Well, it could be that your characters are well drawn, your story compelling, your dialogue sparkling, but the reader goes ballistic over writing mechanics. So, maybe that's something you need to work on. Or perhaps this reader can't abide clichés. Take a look at all of your characters—even the most minor ones—and see if they fall into the "stock character" mode or if clichéd descriptions have crept into your writing ("a chill ran up her spine," or, "he turned beet red," or, "she ate like a pig").

Get back on the horse.

- Don't stop writing—not even for a day.

- Write because you love to write.

- Write because you have to write.

- Write because writing brings you joy.

- Don't ever allow anyone to take that away from you.

DECODING THE REJECTION LETTER

There's another kind of rejection that all writers who are serious about getting published have to deal with: the rejection letter. But here's what you need to keep in mind: if you're not getting rejection letters, that means you're not sending out your work.

The stories are legion of the now iconic authors who sent out their work only to be rejected and rejected and rejected until finally getting published. Where would the literary world be if Stephen King, J. D. Salinger, or Jack Kerouac had given up after a few tries? Indeed, any "normal" person would have thrown in the towel after about the tenth rejection, but these authors tried every avenue, kept plugging away at it until they succeeded. Don't you owe it to yourself to at least try as many times as these authors did?

While the impulse is to toss all rejections in the recycling bin, if you know how to read them right, they can offer you valuable clues to help you get one step closer to getting published.

While the impulse is to toss all rejections in the recycling bin, if you know how to read them right, they can offer you valuable clues to help you get one step closer to getting published. Understand that all rejection letters are not created equal. Some rejection letters can actually offer you a path to success.

Following are the six most common rejection letters—and how to use them to help you move closer to your goal of publication.

1. The "Dear Author" rejection.

This preprinted form letter offers no clues whatsoever as to why your work has been rejected. It may not even be signed. After all the blood, sweat, and tears you poured into your work, to have it responded to almost as if it were a piece of junk mail is infuriating.

Translation: Unfortunately, there is no meaning to glean from this kind of rejection. Ignore it and move on.

2. The "atta boy" rejection.

This can be either jotted by hand or printed at the end of a form letter, offering a nugget of encouragement: "Keep writing," or, "Good writing, but sorry not for us," or, "Great characters," or something else complimentary.

Translation: A hurried reader liked your writing enough to say something nice about it. Use that as fuel to keep sending your work out.

3. The "my heart's not in it" rejection.

This letter will give you some sort of positive response and non-reason for the rejection. Here's an actual example from an author who came to me after receiving a number of rejections: "You have a great imagination—I love the premise—and you're a good writer, but I'm sad to say that I just wasn't passionate enough about this to ask to see more. I wish I could offer constructive suggestions, but I think it's the kind of thing that really is subjective."

Translation: The reader thought enough of your work to craft a personal response and offer a word of encouragement. Keep this agent or publisher in mind for future projects.

4. The "I like it ... but" rejection.

This letter will give some positive feedback and tangible reasons for the rejection. Here's an actual example: "It's clear that you are capable of creating fully fleshed-out characters, and your elegant prose was a pleasure to read. Unfortunately, as a result of slow pacing in the opening chapters I just couldn't get as invested in the book as I would have liked. I'm not the right agent for this book, but I'm grateful for the chance to have read it. I wish you the best of luck in finding the right representation."

Translation: You're almost there. While it can be tricky to know whether the response is purely one of personal taste or bias, reread your manuscript and see if there's any validity to the reader's response. Ask, "What would make the reader more excited? More passionate?" Are you taking enough chances in your writing? Making bold choices? Keep trying. It's just a matter of time before you hit the right agent.

5. The "try again" rejection.

This letter expresses something positive about your work and ends with an invitation, such as, "Please keep us in mind for any future works."

Translation: They like your writing—they really like your writing. This manuscript may not be right for them for a number of reasons. Keep them in mind for future works, and be sure to remind them of this response.

6. The "I'm almost ready to commit" rejection.

This is like being one number off in the million-dollar lottery. The agent or publisher will ask you to fix one or more things before taking on your manuscript. The letter will say something like, "I can't take this on at the time being, but if you … [some specific suggestion here], I'll reconsider."

Translation: "I really like this book, but there are just a few things that bother me about it." Don't let this opportunity slip out of your fingers! Send back a note of thanks, telling the agent you're revising your manuscript according to her directions. If you're not sure how to address what's being asked, hire a professional editor to work with you. A professional editor—preferably one who has had experience working in one of the major book publishing companies—will know exactly how to decipher the agent's comments and guide you to implementing them thoroughly.

DON'T GIVE UP!

Rejection letters are tough to digest. But think of them as necessary for truly uncovering what your manuscript needs to succeed in the market. Try to learn from them what you can, and if you're still not getting any "yesses," then it may be time to bring in an expert. That's what the next chapter is all about.

23

YOUR SECRET WEAPON
The Professional Editor

"I keep hoping I'm done before I actually am, and that's where an editor comes in for me. That's the one person who's objective. If they feel something's missing, it is. If they feel that stuff is being overwritten, then I'm overwriting. It's a leap of faith."

—Richard Price

NO MATTER HOW confident you may be in your story, how enraptured you are with your characters, or how knowledgeable you may feel you are of the publishing world, everyone (even major bestselling authors like Richard Price) needs a second pair of eyes. I'm not just talking about someone to point out inconsistencies or to correct grammar and punctuation. A good editor will help you strengthen your story and characters; a great editor will help you discover your story's hidden genius. But too often, beginning authors feel they can go it alone or rely on the opinions of their writing friends, a former English teacher, the office colleague who's "good with words," or worse, family members. They don't really understand exactly what it is that a professional editor does.

A good editor will help you strengthen your story and characters; a great editor will help you discover your story's hidden genius.

Many years ago, when I was an editor at Random House, it was possible for first-time authors to send their work directly to the publisher to be considered. Most likely, the work would end up in a "slush pile"—a constantly growing tower of manuscript-stuffed cardboard boxes beside an editorial assistant's desk. Among the many other duties, it was the assistant's task to wade through these unsolicited manuscripts and either reject them outright or send them on to an upper-level editor with a recommendation. The harsh reality was that ninety-five percent of those manuscripts ended up being rejected outright. Of the five percent that remained, maybe one percent actually got a deal.

I remember the first deal I made as an editor in the paperback division of Random House. I had discovered this author, Robert D. Bennett III, in the slush pile. He had written a men's action/adventure novel called *Sector 12*. While it was certainly original, and there was a great story in there, it needed a lot of work to heighten the story, develop the characters, and sharpen the prose—not to mention that it was way too long. Fortunately, I had a terrific mentor who I worked under who was willing to let me buy the novel and cultivate this author. It ended up being a great move, because Bennett went on to write a whole series of books.

Unfortunately, a first-time author in a similar situation today would not have such good fortune. Here's the harsh reality of the publishing world: it's harder than ever to get a traditional book deal because publishing houses are buying fewer books than they had in the past and taking fewer chances on untested authors—unless they happen to be celebrities. To add to the problem, staffs have been cut drastically in publishing houses, so the editors left on board are mostly acquiring editors and have scant time to develop new authors.

What that means for you, the first-time author, is that you need to make a great first impression on an agent or publisher if you want to get a deal. The more you can get professional guidance before you start sending out your work, the better shot you'll have at getting a publishing contract.

WHEN TO BRING IN AN EDITOR

Often, authors will get in touch with me after racking up a pile of rejections. In these cases, they see an editor as their last, best hope for turning around their manuscript and getting a book deal. But I'd like you to think a little differently here. Instead of seeing an editor as a second chance to rescue a dying project, think of an editor as your best chance of guiding you to publishing success early in the process.

> Instead of seeing an editor as a second chance to rescue a dying project, think of an editor as your best chance of guiding you to publishing success early in the process.

The kind of editor I'm talking about here is a **developmental editor**. This is an editor who will help you develop your idea into a publishable work, who will help you get the story in place. She will help you make sure your characters are well developed, the structure is sound, and all the other story-telling elements, such as those explored in this book, are in place. Essentially, a developmental editor should be your creative partner.

In my experience, ninety-nine percent of authors—even if they've completed a draft and had it work-shopped—need developmental editing, not just someone to go through and smooth out the writing and fix some errors. Even if you've had your work critiqued by a writing group or writing friends, a developmental editor will pick up on things and offer the kind of guidance that only a true "insider" can offer.

Many of my authors have complete drafts. But what if *you're* not there yet? When's the best time to bring in an editor? Actually, it's never too soon. Often, I have authors who want to get everything "just right" before they'll let an editor look at it. But remember: the editor is on your side and not there to judge you, only to help you. Many times, an editor can help you get your story in place and avoid many of the mistakes that doom manuscripts to the rejection pile, saving you years of writing and rewriting.

The editor is on your side and not there to judge you, only to help you.

Many of my clients come to me with little more than some roughed out chapters and an idea of what they want their novel to be about. We work intensely over a two-day period to map out all the elements in the story, getting the characters fully fleshed out and putting a solid story structure in place. The great thing about working in this way is that these authors are able to avoid some of the obvious traps and clichés that their story could fall into. This collaborative process also helps us to reveal patterns and motifs and thrilling moments that, working alone, the author might never have discovered. Or, it might have taken the author many, many revisions—and years to come to.

Now, I want to emphasize that these novels are entirely my clients'. All I do is help them to ferret out the story they want to tell in the most effective way. A good developmental editor will not try to take over the story or force you into writing it the way she would. Instead, she's like a midwife, helping you to birth the book that's in you. While most professional editors can recognize problems in a manuscript, you want someone to take on the challenge of finding solutions that are right for you.

Frankly, I believe in the old school of book editing, when editors were truly partners with their authors and fostered the creative process. It's what I loved about working with Robert D. Bennett III, and what I love to this day with every author I work with.

FINDING THE RIGHT EDITOR

Recently, while teaching a novel writing workshop at the Cape Cod Writers Conference, I had lunch with a prominent agent. She confided in me her dismay at having steered a potential client to an editor to get the author's work up to snuff to submit to publishers. This was supposedly a top developmental editor, who had many book credits to her name. But after working with the editor, what the author submitted was now almost totally devoid of the uniqueness of his voice. What had started out as a quirky but messy novel, ended up as a dull but well-structured piece.

What happened?

This is the fear that so many authors have when considering whether to hire a developmental editor. They worry about losing their voice, or that the editor will make them eliminate scenes or characters they love or change basic plot elements that don't feel right to them. Most of all, they worry about having their babies wrested from their grasp and forced into something wholly unrecognizable.

As evidenced by the agent's bad experience, these fears are not totally unfounded. Does that mean you should skip hiring an editor? Hardly. What it does mean is that you need to carefully vet any editor you are considering hiring to be sure you are getting an editor who both believes in your vision and can help you carry it out. It is your book and the editor should strike a balance between being firm regarding what changes need to be made without being too intrusive.

Carefully vet any editor you are considering hiring to be sure you are getting an editor who both believes in your vision and can help you carry it out.

First, let's talk a little bit about who NOT to use as an editor. Avoid calling on family members, even if they are published authors or professional editors. Why? First of all, family members know you too well, so it's very hard for them to be objective about what you write. Plus, you get one of two responses: either they think everything you do is great, in which case they're really not helping you, or they don't really see you as an author because they know where you came from. They know where you got that turn of phrase, or who this character is based on, or where you came up with the idea for a scene or plot. In other words: they know too much.

You also may be tempted to enlist the aid of a former college professor or high school English teacher. And while I hold both in high esteem, they may not necessarily be connected to the publishing industry and what it currently looks for in fiction, or they may not know how to work with a budding novelist to get the best work out of you.

Avoid giving your manuscript to the co-worker or colleague who's "good with words." You may get some helpful corrections on punctuation and grammar, but you won't get any useful guidance on making your manuscript publishable.

Some of my authors use beta readers. These are fine for getting a quick take on your manuscript, on whether certain characters are believable or certain plot points make sense. One of my authors, Dale Funk, has had great success in using beta readers because he's been very selective about who he sends to—for instance, law enforcement people to see whether he has his facts right—he doesn't expect much, and more importantly, he has me as his editor to help him know which comments to pay attention to and which to discard. He uses these beta readers as a supplement to a professional editor.

Let's say you've found a couple of candidates to work with. How do you know the person will be the right editor for you? Here are some things to look for:

Does the editor have a professional website?

Ideally, you want to work with an editor who makes his or her living from editing books—not someone who edits as a hobby.

The first sign of a pro is a professionally done website. While bells and whistles and a slick site in no way convey the quality of the editor, you'll be able to tell how seriously the editor takes her work. Especially look to see if the editor has a blog. Read through the posts carefully so that you can get a sense of her thinking. This will help you to see right away if the person is a good match for you.

Also, keep in mind that some terrific editors share sites with others in their "editorial group." The same holds true: see if the site looks professional and if the editors listed on the site have solid credentials.

What credentials does the editor have?

Unlike doctors, lawyers, accountants, and therapists, there are no degrees for editors. That means you'll have to do a little digging to see if the editor has a professional background. Be sure to read the "About" page on the editor's website. You want to see if he has worked for a traditional publisher. Take note of how many years the editor has been in the business. Like most professions, it takes years for editors to hone their skills.

What kind of editing does the editor do?

At this stage, you really want to work with a developmental editor. There are editors who are strictly copy editors, and they are absolutely necessary to the publishing process. A copy editor checks for spelling, grammar, punctuation, consistency, etc. This is the last stage of editing before a manuscript goes to press.

Does the editor specialize in your genre?

Most editors will edit a variety of types of work. But you do want to be sure you're hiring a fiction editor and one who has had experience in your genre.

Does the editor have testimonials from authors she has worked with?

Most likely, you'll find these testimonials on the editor's website, or his *LinkedIn* bio page. Look to see if the authors giving the testimonials have actually had their books published. If all the testimonials are given by people with only first names, they may not be valid. Read the testimonials carefully. They can offer up a big clue as to how the editor works. And don't be afraid to contact the author providing the testimonial. One of my authors did just that when he was considering whether to go with me. That was his way of checking to see if the testimonials were real.

Is the editor willing to talk to you before you commit?

A good editor will want to get a sense of you, the author, and whether you'll be a good fit. This is also a good opportunity to see if you feel comfortable with the editor. Keep in mind that some editors are more analytical, others more fluid in their approach. By speaking to the editor, you will get a feel for his or her style.

Ideally, the editor should be willing to take a look at a few pages to get a sense of your writing and how she can help you. However, do not ask the editor to edit a sample of your work for free. Besides not valuing the editor's time, it really won't tell you anything about how the editor will approach the entire manuscript—only what immediate errors come to mind. That may be okay if you're only looking to hire a copy editor (in that case, offer to pay for the edited sample), but a developmental editor needs to read a full story before offering up suggestions.

Do not ask the editor to edit a sample of your work for free. Besides not valuing the editor's time, it really won't tell you anything about how the editor will approach the entire manuscript— only what immediate errors come to mind.

How does the editor like to work?

Every editor has his own style of approaching a manuscript. Some only want to work with complete manuscripts; others are willing to work with you as you develop your story. Some offer a long "critique letter," others offer their comments in the margins on the manuscript, and still others do both. Some will work with you in person; others do it strictly on paper. There's no right or wrong way, only what feels right for you and what fits in with your needs.

WORKING WITH YOUR EDITOR

Remember: The author/editor relationship is a partnership. To make that partnership work effectively, there are a few simple things for you to keep in mind:

Be open to suggestion.

Listen to what your editor is trying to tell you. After all, you hired him because you valued his expertise. Avoid the temptation to justify your writing choices ("No, you don't understand, the reason I have this in here is because …"). If you have to explain it, it doesn't work.

Avoid bringing in your personal drama.

While the editor/author relationship can often be very close, you want to be careful to keep that closeness within the professional realm. Believe it or not, I had one author say to me, "I have a lump. It may be cancer. You are my last hope. If this book isn't published, I don't know what I'll do." What am I supposed to do with that?

Keep to the schedule you set up with your editor.

This not only helps you make good writing progress, but it respects your editor's time.

Speak up.

Don't hesitate to tell your editor if you feel uncomfortable about anything she's suggesting. You need to feel free to communicate and say what's on your mind. Remember: This is your book, and you have ownership of it.

> ### HOW TO FIND AN EDITOR
>
> Beyond doing a Google search, here are some other ways to find an editor:
> **Look in the Acknowledgements of published books.** Most authors will graciously thank the editor who helped them succeed.
>
> **Attend writing conferences.** Independent editors are often asked to speak at writing conferences. This will give you a great opportunity to meet the prospective editor and get to know her first. I've met many of my author clients this way.
>
> **Get a copy of *Jeff Herman's Guide to Book Publishers, Editors, & Literary Agents.*** This book is the gold standard in the industry for finding publishers, literary agents, and independent editors. Besides finding some great editors in here who have been vetted, you'll learn a lot about the industry, as well as what agents are looking for and how to contact them. The book is updated every two years.

Ideally, your editor should be supportive but not controlling, have a firm hand in guiding you and holding you accountable to your goals, and embrace the collaborative process.

Because it's not just the words on the page that you want fixed—it's the relationship with your editor that will help you succeed.

As a novelist, you have embarked on an exciting, sometimes frustrating, often revelatory journey, one that has no doubt taken you through uncharted territory and rough seas. Not everyone completes the journey. People dream of writing a book, but many do not understand what is needed to actually make the commitment so that their dream becomes a reality.

By now, you should have a fuller understanding of what it takes to write a marketable book—and build yourself as a writer for the long haul. If you've followed the process I've laid out in the previous pages, you can truly be proud when you say, "I wrote my novel."

It has been an honor to guide you.

BOOKS NO WRITER SHOULD BE WITHOUT

BOOKS ON FICTION WRITING

Becoming a Writer
by Dorothea Brande and John Gardner

The Art of Fiction: Notes on Craft for Young Writers
by John Gardner

*The Fire in Fiction: Passion, Purpose,
and Techniques to Make Your Novel Great*
by Donald Maass

*The Breakout Novelist: Craft and Strategies
for Career Fiction Writers*
by Donald Maass

INSPIRATIONAL BOOKS ON WRITING

On Writing: A Memoir of the Craft
by Stephen King

Bird by Bird: Some Instructions on Writing and Life
by Anne Lamott

Zen in the Art of Writing: Essays on Creativity
by Ray Bradbury

The Artist's Way: A Spiritual Path to Higher Creativity
by Julia Cameron

Several Short Sentences About Writing
by Verlyn Klinkenborg

Wild Mind: Living the Writer's Life
by Natalie Goldberg

BOOKS ON PROPER USE OF LANGUAGE

The Elements of Style
by William Strunk, Jr. and E. B. White

Sin and Syntax: How to Craft Wickedly Effective Prose
by Constance Hale

How to Write a Sentence: And How to Read One
by Stanley Fish

Line by Line: How to Improve Your Own Writing
by Claire Kehrwald Cook

BOOKS ON STORY STRUCTURE

The Art of Dramatic Writing: Its Basis in the Creative Interpretation of Human Motives
by Lajos Egri

Story: Substance, Structure, Style,
and the Principles of Screenwriting
by Robert McKee

The Anatomy of Story: 22 Steps
to Becoming a Master Storyteller
by John Truby

BOOKS ON THE CREATIVE PROCESS

Writing on Both Sides of the Brain:
Breakthrough Techniques for People Who Write
by Henriette Anne Klauser

Accidental Genius: Using Writing to Generate
Your Best Ideas, Insight and Content
by Mark Levy

Writing Down the Bones: Freeing the Writer Within
by Natalie Goldberg

BOOKS TO HELP YOU GET PUBLISHED

Don't Sabotage Your Submission:
Insider Information from a Career Manuscript Editor to Save
Your Manuscript from Turning Up D.O.A.
by Chris Roerden

Jeff Herman's Guide to Book Publishers, Editors & Literary
Agents: Who They Are, What They Want, How to Win
Them Over
by Jeff Herman

INDEX

P

Q

R

KEEP IN TOUCH

Thank you for purchasing this book. I hope you have found it helpful. I invite you to keep in touch with me. Here's how:

Visit my website www.WriteToSellYourBook.com to find out how I work with authors, get the latest information on my appearances, and read my blog.

Sign up for my newsletter:
www.WriteToSellYourBook.com/insider-writing-tips

Follow me on twitter:
@WriteToSell

If you'd like me to speak at your next event, please go to:
www.WriteToSellYourBook.com/book-diane-for-events

Made in the USA
San Bernardino, CA
09 November 2017